Putting Your
TALENT
to Work

Other Works by Dr. Lucia Capacchione

Books

The Creative Journal: The Art of Finding Yourself
The Power of Your Other Hand
*The Well-Being Journal: Drawing on Your Inner Power to Heal
      Yourself*
*The Creative Journal for Children: A Guide for Parents, Teachers
      and Counselors*
The Creative Journal for Teens
Light Up Your Body, Lighten Up Your Life (with E. Johnson &
      J. Strohecker)
The Picture of Health: Healing Your Life with Art
Recovery of Your Inner Child
Creating a Joyful Birth Experience (with S. Bardsley)

Audiotapes

The Picture of Health (Meditation & Journal Exercises)
The Wisdom of Your Other Hand (set of five tapes)

For information regarding Dr. Capacchione's books, tapes,
presentations and consultations, contact her at:

Lucia Capacchione
P.O. Box 1355, Cambria, CA 93428
(805) 546-1424

For information about Dr. Van Pelt's lectures and consulting services
contact:

Peggy Van Pelt
Mosaic, Inc., 4720 Canoga Ave., Woodland Hills, CA 91364
(818) 716-1069

PUTTING YOUR TALENT TO WORK

Identifying, Cultivating and Marketing Your Natural Talents

LUCIA CAPACCHIONE, Ph.D.

and

PEGGY VAN PELT, Ph.D.

Health Communications, Inc.
Deerfield Beach, Florida

Grateful acknowledgment is made to the following for permission to reprint the listed copyrighted material:

Ohio University/Swallow Press: Quotations from *The Creative Journal: The Art of Finding Yourself* by Lucia Capacchione. ©1979 Lucia Capacchione.

Newcastle Publishing Co. Inc.: Quotations from *The Power of Your Other Hand* by Lucia Capacchione. ©1988 Lucia Capacchione.

W. W. Norton & Company, Inc. for a quotation on transitions. From *Letters to a Young Poet* by Rainer Maria Rilke, translated by M. D. Herter Norton. Translation copyright 1934, 1954 by W. W. Norton & Company, Inc., renewed ©1962, 1982 by M. D. Herter Norton. Reprinted by permission of W. W. Norton & Company, Inc.

Library of Congress Cataloging-in-Publication Data

Capacchione, Lucia.
    Putting your talent to work : identifying, cultivating and marketing your natural talents / Lucia Capacchione & Peggy Van Pelt.
      p.   cm.
    Includes bibliographical references (p.).
    ISBN 1-55874-406-1 (trade paperback)
    1. Vocational guidance. 2. Vocational interests. I. Van Pelt, Peggy, date.
  II. Title.
  HF5381.C262   1996
  158.6—dc 20   96-25637
                                                    CIP

Publisher: Health Communications, Inc.
              3201 S.W. 15th Street
              Deerfield Beach, FL 33442-8190

Editing & book design: Aleta Pearce
Image management: Philip Wei

TO OUR FAMILIES,
FOR THEIR CONTINUED
LOVE,
ENCOURAGEMENT
AND
SUPPORT

CONTENTS

AUTHORS' PREFACE . . . . **xiii**

ACKNOWLEDGMENTS . . . . **xvii**

GUIDELINES FOR JOURNAL WORK . . . . . . **xix**

PUTTING IDEAS INTO ACTION
ILLUSTRATIONS FOR INSPIRATION
JOURNALING: GIVE YOUR BRAIN A HAND
TIPS FOR JOURNALING
    Time
    Frequency
    Setting
    Confidentiality
    Preparation
MATERIALS YOU WILL NEED
    Talent Journal
    Collage/Mixed Media

Chapter One: IDENTIFYING TALENT 1
Journal and art activities are listed in italics.

WHAT IS TALENT?
THE TRUTH ABOUT TALENT
TALENT IN TODAY'S WORLD
ANCIENT WISDOM
TALENT SEARCH
    The Early Years
    What Do You Want to Be When You Grow Up? (Part 1)
    What Do You Want to Be When You Grow Up? (Part 2)
    What Do You Want to Be When You Grow Up? (Part 3)

Daydreams
If You Can Dream It, You Can Do It
Make Believe
The Magic Wand (Part 1)
The Magic Wand (Part 2)
Having Fun
Go for the Fun
Passion
My Greatest Passions
Ordinary Places
Right Under My Nose (Part 1)
Right Under My Nose (Part 2)
Frustrations
From Frustration to Satisfaction
Crisis
Turning Crisis into Opportunity (Part 1)
Turning Crisis into Opportunity (Part 2)
Transitions
Endings and Beginnings (Part 1)
Endings and Beginnings (Part 2)
Mapping Your Talent (Part 1)
Mapping Your Talent (Part 2)

Chapter Two: ACCEPTING TALENT 53

NON-ACCEPTANCE OF TALENT
    Signs of Non-Acceptance
    Blocks to Accepting Talent
    The Inner Critic
    Rules About Roles
    Confronting the Inner Critic
    The Outer Critic
    Telling It Like It Is (Part 1)
    Telling It Like It Is (Part 2)
    The Critic Turned Inside Out
    Nothing But the Truth (Part 1)
    Nothing But the Truth (Part 2)

SELF-PERCEPTION AND FEAR
SUPPORT FOR TALENT: STRENGTH IN NUMBERS
BOUNDARIES AND LIMITS ON CRITICISM
    Eliminate the Negative
    Finding Support and Setting Boundaries
ACCEPTING YOUR TALENT, EMBRACING A NEW SELF
    Visioning Your Talent at Work
TALENT WORKOUT
    Heart's Desire
    Appointments with Talent
    Talent Review
    Feedback

Chapter Three: DEVELOPING TALENT 89

COURAGE
    Follow Your Heart (Part 1)
    Follow Your Heart (Part 2)
GROWTH
    Visits to the Unknown
RESPECT
    R-E-S-P-E-C-T (Part 1)
    R-E-S-P-E-C-T (Part 2)
    R-E-S-P-E-C-T (Part 3)
PERSISTENCE
    Mapping the Territory, Staying the Course (Part 1)
    Mapping the Territory, Staying the Course (Part 2)
GRATITUDE
    The Talent Fairy Godmother (Part 1)
    The Talent Fairy Godmother (Part 2)
    Taking Time for Talent
TALENT WORKOUT
    Heart's Desire
    Talent Review
    Feedback

Chapter Four:
MATCHING TALENT TO NEEDS 131

COMPLAINTS
  Discovering Needs: Complaint Department
COMPLAINTS OF OTHERS
  Identifying Needs: From Demand to Supply (Part 1)
  Identifying Needs: From Demand to Supply (Part 2)
WISHES
  Filling the Needs: Make a Wish . . . (Part 1)
  Filling the Needs: Make a Wish . . . (Part 2)
  Helping Others
NECESSITY
  Necessity Calls, Talent Answers (Part 1)
  Necessity Calls, Talent Answers (Part 2)
ACTION
TALENT WORKOUT
  Heart's Desire
  Talent Review
  Feedback

Chapter Five:
PUTTING TALENT TO WORK 167

GROWING YOUR CAREER
TALENT AS CAREER COACH
  Talent As Healer and Guide (Part 1)
  Talent As Healer and Guide (Part 2)
WORK STYLE AND CAREER
  What's My Line? (Part 1)
  What's My Line? (Part 2)
THE CAREER COLLECTION
  Jobs, Jobs, Jobs (Part 1)
  Jobs, Jobs, Jobs (Part 2)

WORK IS LOVE
   Working with Love (Part 1)
   Working with Love (Part 2)
REDEFINING CAREER
   If the Truth Be Told
ACTION
TALENT WORKOUT
   Heart's Desire
   Talent Review
   Feedback

Chapter Six:
BEING RESPONSIBLE FOR TALENT . . . 201

ORDER AND CHAOS
THE RULES WE LIVE BY
   Order Out of Chaos (Part 1)
   Order Out of Chaos (Part 2)
RULES AND CHOICES
   Off the Beaten Path
CHANGING RULES
   Rules of the Road
BELIEFS, RULES AND CHOICES
   Mapping the Road, Creating the Rules
RULES ACROSS CULTURES AND GENERATIONS
   Generation Gaps and Cultural Divides
CREATIVITY BETWEEN THE RULES
RULES IN TIMES OF CRISIS
   Crisis and Change
ACTION
TALENT WORKOUT
   Heart's Desire
   Talent Review
   Feedback

Chapter Seven:
MARKETING YOUR TALENT 239

WHAT ARE YOU OFFERING?
  Packaging My Talent
  What I'm Offering
HOW MUCH DO YOU WANT?
WHOM ARE YOU SELLING TO?
MARKETING TO THE NEEDS
  Whom I'm Selling To
REACHING THE MARKET
NETWORKING
  Networking Inventory
A TALENT MENTOR
PERSONAL PRESENTATION
TEAM POWER
  Talent Buddies
    Marketing Support System
  Support Groups
  Starting a Support Group
  Characteristics of a Healthy Support Group
  Structuring Support Group Sessions
  Celebrating
CONGRATULATIONS!

RESOURCES 275

Books
Audiotapes

AUTHORS' PREFACE

We would like to introduce ourselves to you, share our stories and tell you why we wrote this book. On the surface, our early backgrounds are as different as they can be. Peggy, the daughter of a Naval officer, grew up on military bases and seaports throughout the continental United States and Hawaii. Lucia was raised in Los Angeles, capital of the movie and television industries that employed her parents. We traveled in very different circles and lived worlds apart, but inside we were very much alike. The first time we met, we knew our paths had been destined to cross. Here is Peggy's recollection of her earliest years:

Traveling as much as the family did meant that I had to amuse myself on long trips from one location to another. My first memories were of drawing and creating handcrafts with my three brothers. I especially remember the Halloween we celebrated when I was three years old. My mother made a pumpkin princess costume for me. I fell in love with it and I have spent the rest of my life "dressing up," including careers as a costume designer and artist.

My work path was also influenced by an early discovery in my teens: teaching art to neighborhood kids paid more than baby-sitting. At the same time, I found that I was a good organizer for family events, a role in which my family has continued to cast me. It is clear that all of this was early training for a life in the entertainment industry: theme parks, film, television, theater and performance art. As a 25-year staff member with the Disney organization, I have done everything from costuming bears and feathering birds to being the talent developer for a world-class team of creative professionals in the arts, architecture and engineering.

During Lucia's early years, both parents worked at MGM studios. Her father was a film editor on classic 1940s musicals starring Judy Garland, Gene Kelly and Fred Astaire; her mother was a dress-maker in the wardrobe department. Like Peggy, Lucia learned to amuse herself early in life but for a different reason; she was an only child. As she recalls:

> The very first memory I have is sitting in a high chair at about one year of age and playing with a toy consisting of plastic disks in rainbow colors strung on a chain. I'm sure that my fascination with this toy had an impact on my early interest in art and eventually on my career direction. Fortunately, my interests were nurtured by my family.

> At 21, I graduated from college with a degree in art and launched my first career as a designer of prints, posters, greeting cards and toys characterized by bright colors. One "talking toy" that I developed even taught pre-school children to name colors with "talking disks" (miniature records) that inserted into a little playback machine.

Although we grew up in different environments, there were some common threads. We both endured military settings; for Peggy it was the U.S. Navy, for Lucia it was parochial schools. This world of uniforms and strict rules catalyzed a counter-force, pushing us toward creative expression.

As we began working on this book together, we came across another common bond. In early religious training (Lucia was taught by nuns, Peggy by Protestant Sunday school teachers), we had both been impressed by the Bible story about the talents as told by Matthew (25:14-30):

> A man went on a long journey and entrusted three of his servants with talents (of money). To one he gave five talents, to another two talents and to the third he gave one, each according to his abilities. While the master was away, the man with five talents put the money to work and doubled it, making it ten. The man with two talents did the same. But the third man hid his talent, burying it in the ground.

> When their master returned and saw that the first two men had doubled the talents, he was pleased. "Well done, good and faithful servant," he said to them. He rewarded them with more responsibility and invited them to share his happiness. When the man who had buried his talent reported what he had done, the master was displeased. This servant had wasted the opportunity to let the talent bear fruit. He ordered the talent be given to the man with ten talents, saying: "Everyone who has will be given more, and he will have an abundance." Finally, he said, "Throw that worthless servant out into the darkness."

In our young minds, we understood the word "talent" to mean abilities or gifts. From hearing this story we both came to the same conclusion: talents *must* be used. This dictum had the ring of truth and the weight of divine proclamation. We took it very seriously. Talents were not to be ignored or frittered away. They were to be cultivated, multiplied and shared. Both of us have lived our lives by this rule and it has served us well. It is the premise and foundation of this book.

Peggy's interest in guiding the careers of others stemmed from her fascination with how talent and creativity were reflected in her own career. She also observed hundreds of incredibly talented peers in the entertainment industry. They each had their own unique way of approaching work. Her commitment to fostering creativity led her to become a talent development specialist.

Lucia's career counseling work happened almost by accident. A mid-life crisis ushered in a new career as an art therapist. It was a perfect blend of her experience as an artist and a child development specialist. After being in private practice for a few years, an unexpected thing happened. Her clients wanted to know how to make career changes.

"It's simple," she told them. "Listen to the voice of talent within; find your natural abilities and interests. Ask yourself what you love doing the most and figure out how you can make a living doing it." Before long, she was receiving lots of referrals for creative career counseling.

It was many years later that we met and the fun really began. After working together for 10 years in corporate settings, we decided to gather our collective information and write it down. We found that our careers had been driven by our talent. It is not surprising that when writing about talent, we spoke in one voice.

In developing this book, it became clear to us that a talent-based career is fast becoming the "way of the 21st century." We welcome you to a great adventure: the journey to find, cultivate and share your innate talents.

ACKNOWLEDGMENTS

Many people gave generously of their time in helping us create this book. Special thanks go to those professionals who field-tested the exercises in this book and gathered illustrations and journal examples:

Mary Becker
Hannelore Hutton, MFCC
Evvie Moravec
Mariellen O'Hara, Ph.D.
Judy O'Keefe, Career Counselor

Our heartfelt appreciation goes to all those who contributed the journal writings, drawings and collages that enliven these pages:

Joe Airo
Jim Barry
Mary Becker
Kay Bliss
Dee Crowley
Eve Edwards
Verne Edwards
Jim Elliott
Linda Lee
Jan Moore
Evvie Moravec
Mariellen O'Hara
Judy O'Keefe

ACKNOWLEDGMENTS

Bill Osmon
Dean Pappas
Aleta Pearce
Anitra Redlefsen
Chuck Salomon
Connie Snyder
Russell Tavaglione
Bob Van Pelt
Wally Van Pelt
Christopher West
Clay Whittaker

Very, very special thanks to our editor and designer, Aleta Pearce, for her tireless and dedicated work on all aspects of this project. Without her contribution you would not be holding this book in your hands.

To Philip Wei, we extend our appreciation for the use of his studio, equipment and expertise in preparing the artwork for reproduction.

Our gratitude also goes to Peter Vegso, our publisher, for his faith in the project, and to Gary Seidler of U.S. Journal Training for bringing us into the Health Communications family. Thanks also to Christine Belleris, editor at Health Communications, and her staff for their support.

GUIDELINES FOR JOURNAL WORK

PUTTING IDEAS INTO ACTION

To help you take action and put your talent to work, we have made this an interactive book. It is a book **to do** instead of just to read. For inspiration, we've included concrete examples from the lives of people who have successfully created handmade, custom-tailored careers that fit them like a glove. Their stories are followed by fun and easy journal activities for you to do.

ILLUSTRATIONS FOR INSPIRATION

Each activity is illustrated with inspiring drawings and writings contributed by people who keep a Talent Journal. These examples are in their own special borders that simulate journal pages. A note of caution: these illustrations are meant to inspire you, not to be copied. As the great Japanese poet Basho once said, "We do not seek to imitate the masters; rather, we seek what they sought." In using this book you will be seeking what other successful career-makers have sought: how to use all their talents. There are no right or wrong ways to do the journal activities in this book. There is only *your* way.

JOURNALING: GIVE YOUR BRAIN A HAND

In this book, you'll be developing your creativity by writing and drawing with both your dominant and non-dominant hands. Dialogs written with both hands have proved to be a highly effective technique for accessing the emotional, creative Inner Child self and bringing it to the awareness of the adult self. These dialogs are also an excellent means for activating the *corpus callosum* and opening up communication between both hemispheres of the brain. This literally allows the non-verbal right brain to know what the left brain is thinking and feeling. For more techniques on accessing your Inner Child, see Lucia's book, *Recovery of Your Inner Child*. The chapters on the Playful Child and Creative Child are especially relevant for exploring talent.

Human beings have two hands.
One hand is called dominant, the other has
    no name.
One hand is defined by what it can do,
    the other by what it cannot do.
One hand is trained and educated,
    the other is ignored and unschooled.
One hand writes, the other is illiterate.
One hand is skilled, the other is awkward.
One hand is powerful, the other is weak.
No matter which hand is dominant, right or
    left, the same internal politics exist.
One has the "upper hand," the other is "left
    out."

As far as we know, individual humans have always had a dominant hand. We accept handedness unquestioningly as being "in the nature of things." We expect it to be so and we teach it to our children. As soon as the infant feeds itself or grabs a toy, we encourage or coerce it to prefer one hand. Later, the child scribbles, draws pictures and eventually learns to write its own name with the dominant hand.

Lucia Capacchione, from *The Power of Your Other Hand*

With few exceptions, everyone writes and draws exclusively with one hand, including the ambidextrous. We call our writing hand the dominant hand. The other hand performs "unskilled labor," playing a supporting role. This is referred to as the non-dominant hand. In fact, this is how we define handedness. Whether we realize it or not, using only one hand for writing profoundly impacts the way we think and use our brains.

The brain has two symmetrical sides that look alike but don't act alike. The left side of the brain contains centers that specialize in verbal and mathematical reasoning, logic and sequential organization. The ability to read, write, do math, analyze and schedule time are all left-brain functions. Professions that rely heavily on left-brain functioning are accounting, law, editing and engineering. By selecting and training one hand to write, we hard-wire that hand to the verbal side of the brain. This is true whether we are right or left-handed.

By contrast, the right hemisphere specializes in visual/spatial perception, enabling us to recognize familiar faces, places and things. There are centers in the right brain that allow us to navigate and orient ourselves in the environment. Having a good sense of direction is an attribute of this right-brain function. Art, dance, architecture and design are highly right-brain professions. In addition, the right brain is associated with emotional expressiveness, intuitive abilities and spiritual experiences (such as meditation) that have the quality of timelessness. Imagination, visualization and metaphoric thought are all made possible by the right brain. The non-rational right hemisphere allows for breakthrough thinking, inventions, innovations in any field of activity. Lucia's research shows that writing and drawing with the non-dominant is a direct route for accessing the capabilities of the right brain.

Connecting the two hemispheres of the brain is a bundle of nerve fibers known as the *corpus callosum*. Metaphorically speaking, the *corpus callosum* is a bridge between two worlds, between the rational and intuitive, the logical and emotional, the functional and esthetic. True creativity relies on the use of both sides of the brain. Right-brain flights of imagination need left-brain structure to ground them and make them a physical reality. The activities in this book will help you develop the brain's little-used right hemisphere. In this way you can balance both sides of the brain equally, letting the left side of your brain know what the right side is thinking.

TIPS FOR JOURNALING

Throughout this book, we recommend activities to be done in a Talent Journal. The following are some tips for journaling:

Time

When doing journal work, it is important to block out some uninterrupted time. Some activities in this book take 15 minutes, others take more. We have divided some into parts so that you can do each one at a different sitting.

Frequency

You don't have to do these activities every day. When and how long you spend working in your journal is up to you. The more journal work you do, the greater the benefits you will receive. However, frequency and duration of journal sessions are your choice.

Setting

The best setting for journal work is a place that is conducive to concentration and self-reflection. We recommend a quiet, comfortable place where you can be alone and undistracted. Some people like to start the day off doing these activities. Others prefer to sit in bed before going to sleep at night and do some journaling.

Many people tell us they have a favorite spot in nature or a special place at home where they go to journal. Wherever you are, be sure that you feel safe and that no one will interrupt you.

Confidentiality

Your journal work should be private. Keep your Talent Journal in a safe, private place. If you share your journal entries with others, do it selectively. Share only what you feel comfortable sharing and only with people who are genuinely supportive. Never show journal work to people who are critical or pessimistic about your talent. Avoid those who judge the whole idea of developing talent as the basis for a career. Don't let anyone rain on your parade.

Preparation

When you are ready to begin, sit quietly for a moment and breathe deeply. Relax and let go of any tension or anxiety you are carrying in your body and mind. If fear or doubt comes up, just be aware of it. If your feelings are strong, you can write about them in your journal before going on to do the activity in the book. It is common for people to feel a bit nervous before embarking on the journey to find talent. Doubt and fear may arise. *What if I don't find any talent? What if I do find a lot of talent, then what? Is it going to mean a lot of responsibility? Will others accept my talent? How will this change my life, my relationships, my job?* If these thoughts come up, just write about them. Then go on with the suggested activity. Begin the first page of each Talent Journal entry with the day's date.

When you start writing or drawing with your non-dominant hand, the printing may seem very awkward and slow. The perfectionist in you may come jumping out and criticize you for writing so badly. "This is horrible handwriting," it might say. "Yukkk, look at those mistakes in spelling and grammar; what's wrong with you?" Your dominant hand may try to grab the pen because it can write so much faster and better. Just remember, you're not engaging in any race here, nor are you being tested or given grades. Rather, you are opening up the right side of your brain.

MATERIALS YOU WILL NEED

To do the Talent Journal and art activities suggested in this book, you will need some simple materials:

Talent Journal

- Blank book with unlined white paper, preferably 8½ x 11 (available in bookstores, stationery stores or art supply shops)
- A set of felt pens in 12 or more colors

Collage/Mixed Media

You will also be doing some activities requiring magazine photos.

- Art paper (18" x 24" or larger). We recommend white drawing paper (80 lb.) or poster board (same size as above).
- Scissors
- White glue (Wilhold, Lepages, etc.) or Liquitex "acrylic medium varnish" or "matte medium" (must be applied with a brush). This is like a thick liquid decoupage glue.
- Magazines with photos (*Life*, fashion magazines, travel, architecture, homes and gardens)
- Colored felt pens
- OPTIONAL: Crayons, oil pastels or any other art materials you like to work with

CHAPTER ONE

IDENTIFYING TALENT

WHAT IS TALENT?

The dictionary definitions of talent are:

- a unit of weight or money
- to lift up
- the natural endowments of a person or a special (often creative or artistic) aptitude
- a general intelligence or mental power

These definitions suggest **a fundamental connection between our inherent capabilities, the ability to be inspired and to make money**. This connection between talent, inspiration and money is the premise upon which we have based this book.

THE TRUTH ABOUT TALENT

When people hear the word talent, they often respond by saying, "I don't have any." Many people associate talent exclusively with the arts and sports: the ability to draw, sing, dance, perform, write, hit a home run, make a touchdown, slam dunk a basketball, etc.

MYTH: Only a few people are talented.
FACT: Every human being is born with unique gifts and talents.

Talent can be found in all areas of life; it knows no boundaries. It is an innate human characteristic. *Particular* talents are unique to each individual, but talent is *universal*. We all have it. Talent can express itself in virtually all activities: ordinary routines, hobbies, volunteer work, career, etc. Talent is what drives:

- The enthusiastic botany student considered a "born scientist."
- The woman with a "flair" for fashion and accessorizing.

- The bookkeeper with a "knack" for number crunching.
- The working mother with a "genius" for balancing career and parenting.
- The proofreader who can "spot a missing period from across the room."
- The girl known as a "natural" for taking care of young children.
- The handyman with the "gift" for fixing anything.
- The waitress with an "innate aptitude" for satisfying customers.
- The computer whiz kid who can do the "impossible."

MYTH: Other people are talented but I'm not.
FACT: Every human being is born with unique gifts and talents, including you.

This book focuses on how to let talent guide your career. To have a talent-based career you must find, accept and develop your innate gifts. Once you've done this, you can then share your talent by applying it to needs.

Most of us feel we may have at least one talent that we can name. The truth is that we are all multi-talented. The question is: "Where can I find my talents?" This book answers that question.

TALENT IN TODAY'S WORLD

We are living in a world filled with explosive and unpredictable changes. All the old rules have lost their meaning. Our former arch enemy, the Soviet Union, no longer exists in that definition. The "American Dream," the nuclear family in a suburban house with a white picket fence, has been reduced to TV sitcom reruns. Generation X is the first post-World War II generation to fall from economic "grace." Upward mobility has ceased to be the national birthright. "America the beautiful" is being assaulted by natural and man-made disasters with record-breaking frequency.

The good news is that a new spirit is being born. It is a spirit of creativity and entrepreneurship. An increasing number of people have grown tired of waiting for the "boss," corporation or government to take care of them. They are learning to trust their own abilities, experience and inner direction. Technology has led to a sharp increase in home-based businesses. People are striking out on their own, out of choice or necessity.

ANCIENT WISDOM

In trying to understand what to do about the American economy, a group of business leaders held a conference in the early 90s that our associate, Eleanor McCulley, attended. There were a wide variety of speakers noted for their achievements and success. Much to Eleanor's surprise, there were two Canadian aboriginal women in this group, both leaders in their respective tribes. Edna Manitowabi is an elder and teacher in both the Ogibway and Odawa Nations. Miriam Younchief, an elder in the Kahawin First Nations, is an organizational developer.

These two respected leaders were eminently qualified to address the theme of "valuing people and environment," a key concern of the conference. The conference proposed the question: "What is the next step for American business?" Standing before this impressive group of executives, these aboriginal women said: "We are unable to answer." They further explained: "No one can tell us what actions to take. Each of us needs to discover this on our own. **First, we must know who we are and second, how we behave. Then we will know what actions to take. We will not have to ask what to do. We will simply do it.**"

When Eleanor told us this story, we were deeply moved. We found that these aboriginal women articulated what we had discovered: the best foundation for a career is self-knowledge and the expression of talent.

TALENT SEARCH

What are your talents? How do you find them? Talent is found in many places: your past experience, your imagination and your heart. Once you identify your talent, it belongs to you. Naming talent is the crucial first step in creating your career path. So let's go on a treasure hunt in search of your talent.

The Early Years

As children, we explored our talent in play. We expressed our talent when we played make believe, dressed up or engaged in other activities that allowed free rein to our imagination. We tried on many roles and experimented with different abilities and parts of our personality.

Some individuals are fortunate enough to have discovered their innate gifts at a very early age. They knew exactly what they wanted to be when they grew up. In fact, one organizational development expert, Dr. Will McWhinney, believes that we find the seeds of a fulfilling career in our very first memories. Some professionals we have interviewed told us that their career path was evident as early as 6 or 7 years of age. They simply followed their childhood dreams. Lucia's father is a case in point.

> The year was 1916, the setting, a small remote village in southern Italy. Five-year-old Francesco ventured out one evening expecting to mingle with fellow villagers on their customary after-dinner walk. Much to the boy's surprise, on this particular evening the streets were deserted. Wandering

down to the local stable he saw an unusual sight. The heavy wooden door was ajar and strange flickering lights were spilling out onto the street. The little boy sweet-talked his way past a huge man selling tickets at the entrance.

Inside the darkened stable he could barely make out the silhouettes of seated villagers. They were looking at a white bed sheet hanging on the wall. Behind the villagers was a huge noisy machine projecting light across the room onto the sheet. The light from the machine appeared to be creating pictures that moved on the sheet. What is more, the pictures were telling stories: men in battle scenes, crowds on busy city street scenes, couples embracing. The story and dialog were told in captions. Having never seen a movie before, Francesco was hypnotized. This was the first motion picture ever to be shown in their village. The "miracle" of this light machine making pictures move on the stable wall was an impression that would be with him forever.

Afterward Francesco ran home excitedly to tell his mother and sister what he had seen. His final statement was: *Mama, someday I'm going to make those things. Someday I'm going to make those pictures that move on the wall.* Her wise response was, *If you set your heart on it, you will do it.*

The rest of Francesco's life was an unfoldment of his early childhood dream. After the family's immigration to Los Angeles six years later, fate conspired to make the boy's vision into a reality. Jobs as an usher in movie theaters led to a series of positions at MGM Studios, where he finally became a film editor. Frank, as he was later known, became a pioneer in the television industry, with film editing credits including *The Lone Ranger, Gilligan's Island, The Wild Wild West* and *The Brady Bunch.*

This is a perfect example of a childhood dream come true. Once the vision was clear, Francesco followed it with tenacity and complete conviction. Fortunately, he was in the right place at the right time. Also, his mother continued to encourage her son to follow his dream.

By contrast, there are those who entertained career dreams in childhood but were discouraged or somehow blocked from pursuing their heart's desire. Miyoko's story is a good example of this. Today, at age 38, she is a successful doctor of Oriental medicine, but the route to realizing her dream was a circuitous one.

> As a child growing up in San Francisco, Miyoko was an excellent student and wanted to become a physician when she grew up. Her mother, speaking from an earlier generation, told her that this was an impossible dream. "You would have to compete with men," the mother admonished little Miyoko, "and you would never find a husband." Then Miyoko set her sights on becoming a lawyer. Again her mother discouraged her, warning that, "Men don't like girls who are too smart."
>
> Still wanting to pursue her original interest in the medical field, Miyoko became a nurse. Her mother approved. Although Miyoko was popular with the patients and highly respected in her field, she was miserable. She wanted to be able to do more for her patients than dispense medication, take temperatures and do paperwork. A voracious reader and researcher, Miyoko discovered many alternative approaches to healing. Her presentation of some of these ideas to the hospital staff was met with ridicule. She quickly grew tired of taking a back seat to doctors and hospital administrators.
>
> The situation eventually became so stressful that Miyoko sought therapy. With her therapist's help, Miyoko uncovered her early dream of becoming a doctor. After several weeks it became clear to Miyoko that a career change was in order. She took action and sought career counseling. There she revived her childhood desire to become a doctor and received support to make it a reality. Continuing her exploration, Miyoko discovered that she was attracted to acupuncture. After much soul-searching, this determined young woman decided to go back to school and become a doctor of Oriental medicine.

Miyoko is one of the lucky ones. She may have taken a detour, but she finally lived out her childhood wish.

Although we are adults, there is a creative child that still lives in us. We call it the Inner Child. This child will never grow up and go away. The Inner Child contains our feelings, playfulness and creativity. The child within knows how to daydream and explore possibilities. Our childlike imagination and vision enable us to fulfill our fondest dreams. Unfortunately, when we become adults we often forget how to explore the way we did as kids. The three-part journal activity that follows will help revive your childlike sense of adventure. It is adapted from an exercise in Lucia's earlier book, *The Creative Journal.* As with other journal activities you will be doing, this one is accompanied by an example from someone's talent journal.

What Do You Want to Be When You Grow Up? (Part 1)

MATERIALS: Talent Journal and felt pens

1. Go back into your early memories and ask yourself: "What did I want to be when I grew up?" In your mind, review the years from childhood to adolescence. Remember all the things you wanted to become (or pretended you were) no matter how 'far out' or silly they seem to you now. For example, young children sometimes want to be animals, mythical or fictitious characters and the like.

2. With your non-dominant hand (the hand you don't normally write with), make a list in your journal. Jot down all your childhood and adolescent fantasies about what you wanted to become when you reached adulthood.

What Do You Want to Be When You Grow Up? (Part 2)

MATERIALS: Talent Journal and felt pens

1. Read over the list you made in Part 1 and check off the fantasies that you actually did live out. (You may not have made a career of some of these items, but may have experienced them in some way.)

2. Put an asterisk by the items that you haven't lived out or experienced.

3. Look at the asterisked items again. About each one, ask yourself: "Why didn't I live this wish out? Was there a parental or social pressure against it? Did I lose interest in it? Was it too far out? Was it off limits for boys or girls to pursue that dream?" Next to each item on your list, with your dominant hand, write out the reason that your dream did not become a reality.

I don't remember really thinking about this until junior high school, when counselors began directing me toward sciences. I was attracted to hairdressing & cosmetology, but my grades were good so they sent me to science. I suppose that I might have always wondered if I was smart enough for science so I've satisfied that. Now (many years later) I find myself drawn to the healing arts, psychology, aromatherapy. They seem to soothe my soul.

Why didn't I go straight to my interests?

Teachers didn't value this (hairdressing & cosmetology) and I wanted to please my external world. I had no idea that I might have known better.

I had a career in science that sort of ran its course. Now I'm back to psychology and healing. Dancing wasn't available to me—no money for classes. Music was not available either. Now I teach aerobic dance and buy lots of music. Listen to music all the time.

What Do You Want to Be When You Grow Up? (Part 3)

MATERIALS: Talent Journal and felt pens

1. On a new page (using your dominant hand), make a current list of things that you would like to do or experience during the rest of your life. Include qualities or skills that you want to develop, things that you want to accomplish. You can include or modify unrealized things from your list in Part 1 if they are still pertinent.

2. Go back and put numbers in the left margin, prioritizing your list in order of importance.

What would I like to do in my life?
Work in a beautiful, peaceful, healing environment with soft music, love, enthusiasm and my dog. Play the piano. Fitness director, personal trainer, therapeutic touch/aroma therapist. Feel I'm helping people.

Daydreams

Many people find themselves staring vacantly into space while viewing fantasy stories and situations in their minds. Most people think that daydreams are a waste of time, non-productive, escapist or a sign of mental disturbance. Of course, if most of one's life is lived in daydreams, any or all the above may be true.

On the other hand, daydreams have been a seedbed for some of the greatest contributions to humanity. Volumes have been written about great inventions and breakthroughs in science that were hatched in reveries or daydreams. One of the most famous of these examples is Einstein's discovery of the theory of relativity.

We have interviewed people in all disciplines and asked them: "Where do you get your best ideas?" A large percentage told us that their ideas came during states of absent-mindedness, trance-like relaxation, fantasy, waking up or falling asleep. Very few of them were sitting at a computer, working in their offices or otherwise engaged in their discipline "like a good little professional." These moments of genius have happened while showering, driving on the freeway, washing the dinner dishes, walking in the park, meditating or picnicking. Since daydreaming is such a fertile field, it can yield important information about what your true heart's desire is.

If You Can Dream It, You Can Do It

MATERIALS: Talent Journal and felt pens

1. Reflect on your typical daydreams.

   • Where are you in these daydreams?
   • What are you doing?

- Who are you with?
- How do you feel?

2. Using your non-dominant hand, draw a favorite daydream in your journal.

3. With your dominant hand, write out your thoughts about the images.

   - What is the daydream telling you about your true heart's desire?
   - If your daydream came true, what abilities or personality traits would be developed?
   - What would you accomplish and how would you feel about yourself?

A daydream I have all the time when I preview or show homes (to prospective clients): It's about redoing houses and making them into something wonderful.

I dream of taking this ugly dark home and redoing it totally. And which tradesmen I would call to do this and that. The finished result is a very happy cheerful house, very appealing and cute.

I feel a sense of accomplishment and am very happy and satisfied with the results. Other benefits I'm receiving: learning more and more about the different trades involved with building, cost-effectiveness... how to do it more quickly and move onto the next redressing.

My skill of coordinating and managing projects is being expressed. My talent for seeing how things could be is expressed. How you can transform something and help it and improve it. I'm also expressing my awareness for what is appealing at the time. In this job as career I'm learning to trust myself. I'm learning to rely on myself and take responsibility and credit for a project. I have a boundless amount of energy and enthusiasm and creative talent when let go or unleashed.

Make Believe

While conducting a seminar on creative problem-solving for managers in a major service corporation, Peggy polled the audience. "How many of you feel that you are creative?" she asked. Out of 40 managers, only one raised her hand. As Peggy recalls:

I was utterly amazed at the response to my question. I had been told that all those attending were creative and that I could present advanced material. As soon as I saw that one timid hand and 39 blank stares, I knew that the material would not work. To make matters worse, my seminar had been chosen by the company to be reviewed by the program directors. I thought to myself, "This is a problem and it needs a creative solution."

I had already passed out the advanced material, so I elected to call it "take-home reading." I then launched into the basic elements of creative problem-solving. The group was having a very difficult time. They became more frustrated with each exercise. I repeatedly simplified the material, trying to relieve their frustration. By the end of the seminar we were at a stalemate. They were not getting the material and I was now as frustrated as they were.

A voice in my head kept saying, "Don't give up. Trust the creative process. Be still, and listen to them." With less than a minute left in the seminar, I stood quietly listening and trusting while they struggled with the last exercise. Somewhere in the back of the room I heard a woman sheepishly say to her associate, "I think she wants us to pretend." Yes, that is exactly what I wanted. I asked the woman to repeat her comment. When she repeated it to the group, they got the message. In creative problem-solving you have to *pretend* that alternative strategies are possible. Otherwise you will see only the obvious and the routine solutions as being viable.

I hadn't realized that this group needed permission to pretend. I have never forgotten the lesson. Creative problem-solving is absolutely dependent on the ability to pretend. We all have it. In fact, it is our birthright as human beings. If we have concluded that pretending is childish, deceitful or impractical, then, as adults, we need to give ourselves permission to pretend the way we did as kids.

The Magic Wand (Part 1)

MATERIALS: Talent Journal and felt pens

1. Imagine that the Talent Fairy Godmother appears to you and presents you with a magic wand. "With this magic wand," she says, "you will have the power to create the job or career that is perfect for you. This wand removes all obstacles, breaks through all blocks, dissolves all self-doubts and opens your imagination up

to your true heart's desire." She closes by telling you that, "The perfect job or career is yours for the asking. What will it be?"

2. With your non-dominant hand, draw a picture of yourself in the perfect job or career. In your picture, show where you are, what you are doing, and if you are alone or with others.

3. On the next page, with your dominant hand write about your perfect job or career as shown in your picture. Describe the setting and what you are doing.

- How do you feel about yourself and your work?
- What talents and skills are you expressing?
- What are you learning on this job or in this career?
- How much do you get paid?
- What other benefits are you receiving?

The perfect job has absolutely no deadlines or time clocks on a regular basis. I would love to get into my car and take my camera to wherever my spirit takes me . . . mountains, fields of wildflowers. To capture a moment in time in a photograph . . . wow. Even studio photography would be okay sometimes. I don't want to be trapped indoors!! Taking pictures of children playing would be great. I love my work and I capture emotion, serenity or passion of "the moment," I am very well paid for my work.

I love the idea of "making a memory" and locking it in on the film. I am not trapped by anything.

I guess I must be a freelance photographer. I can go to places I have seen before and explore new places. I will meet people and capture them in film, showing playing, working, joy and sorrow. I get to share in people's lives and experiences. I am living my life . . . truly living. I am free. I am making beautiful mementos of people, places and things to share that will live on and on.

The Magic Wand (Part 2)

MATERIALS: Talent Journal and felt pens

1. Project yourself into the future. You decide how far; three years, five years or more. You are already established in your perfect job or career. Imagine that you are being interviewed by a magazine or newspaper reporter about how you achieved success.

2. Using both hands, write the interview out. Write the reporter's questions with your dominant hand and your responses with the non-dominant hand. The reporter asks the following questions (*Note: If you think of any other questions, you may add them to this list*):

    *   What do you do in your work?
    *   How did you get interested in this line of work?
    *   How did you get where you are today?
    *   What do you like best about what you do?
    *   Are there things that you don't like about your work?
    *   What is the secret to your success?
    *   What advice would you give to someone entering this line of work?

Project yourself into the future.

I am a successful university professor, teaching business courses focusing on insurance, and enjoying the campus community.

What do you do in your work?

I help people learn about what they need. I teach policy, how to run agencies and businesses, accounting, managing.

How did you get interested in this line of work?

I got a master's in human behavior and got interested in people's preferences, especially their communication style.

I became interested in education in the second grade. I went to the library and read a book on Daniel Boone. I've read ever since and loved it. I love learning.

How did you get where you are today?

Hard work, learning a lot in insurance,

listening to my clients, letting them teach me what they do and what they need. Caring about people.

What do you like best about what you do?

The lights go on. Seeing understanding. Seeing people accomplish their goal.

Are there things that you don't like about your work?

Wouldn't want to teach junior high. I was too much a rebel at that age myself.

What is the secret to your success?

Wanting to learn. Teaching because I want to. Wanting others to be successful.

What advice would you give?

Make it exciting for people to learn; then teaching is easy. You get excited, they get excited.

Having Fun

We find talent at the heart of fun-making. Unfortunately, many people think that they can't make a living by having fun. Traditionally, fun and work have been separated. We think that we have to "pay dues" in our work, so that we can have fun in our free time. Sadly, many people never do find fun in work. You don't have to be one of them.

Many of our innate talents come into play when we are enjoying hobbies, avocations and other leisure activities. The talents we exercise while we're having fun can be turned into a career path. We met a successful landscaper who told us how she started as an amateur gardener:

> Cassy's pride and joy was her garden. The mother of two young children, she spent hours with her family planting flowers, vegetables and fruits. Her neighbors, admiring her hard work and beautiful results, asked for advice about their gardens. She was flattered because she thought of herself as "just an amateur."
>
> When her husband was in an accident and went on disability, Cassy needed to earn money to supplement their income. She resumed a former career as a real estate broker and was doing quite well. The more she did it, though, the more unhappy she felt. There was very little time for her real love: gardening. When people commented on her success in real estate, Cassy would say, "I paint a picture in words of the potential that each house has. I point out to potential buyers how (with just a few changes and some creative landscaping) they could improve the property and have a more beautiful home." Every time she said this, Cassy wished she could design these gardens instead of just making suggestions.
>
> Eventually, Cassy decided to stop selling real estate and try her hand at a landscaping business. To her delight, she got clients immediately. When we met her, she was making a handsome living as a landscape designer and having tremendous fun doing it.

Go for the Fun

MATERIALS: Talent Journal and felt pens

1. Have you ever turned fun-making activities or hobbies into an income source? Do you know anyone who has? If you have, using your dominant hand, write down what you did for fun and profit. If you know others who have, interview them and find out how they did it.

    *   How did you get the idea that you could make money doing something you really enjoyed?
    *   How did you go about getting paid for it?

2. Using your non-dominant hand, make a list of fun-making activities in which you are currently involved.

3. Next to each item, brainstorm some ideas for how you can be paid for any of these fun activities, or how you can integrate these activities into your existing job or career.

I loved to go to garage sales and find collectibles or antiques at a reasonable price. I'm not sure how, whether someone suggested it or if I thought of it, but I started setting up at the Flea Market in Omaha the last Sunday of every month. I made a very small profit but was able to pick myself up some nice pieces of furniture for the house. I actually furnished most of the house at a reasonable cost with good furniture. Also, when we moved and I looked for a house myself, I learned a lot about my current job in real estate.

Fun-making activities	How to be paid
Teaching Aerobics	Enlarge classes, more dance classes
Reading	Edit, proofread
Walking my dog	Dog-walking service

Passion

We find talent in passion. In fact, passion feeds talent. Passion is a powerful energy that ignites and engages our love and joy. It is a source of vitality—physical, emotional and mental. Passion seeks expression through our talents. It motivates us to act. Passion reveals who we are, how we behave and what actions we take.

Peggy had the pleasure of working with Sandra, an actress who recognized that she had two great passions: acting and science. Sandra found it difficult to follow a dual career path as a professional actress and a working scientist. It was easier to be a working actress and a student of science. When theater began to falter in the mid 1980s, she decided to combine her theater background and science.

Sandra discovered that she knew how to design and produce events, lectures, seminars and conferences. She could cast people in appropriate roles and facilitate the needs of talented people. In addition, she had a gift for innovative thinking and an ability to grasp complex theory and highly technical language. Sandra discovered that many scientists and artists wanted to exchange ideas with each other. She put her two great passions together and formed an internationally recognized "think tank." Passion clearly marks our talents for us.

My Greatest Passions

MATERIALS: Talent Journal and felt pens

1. With your non-dominant hand, make a list of all the things you feel most passionately about. This can include any aspect of your life.

2. With your non-dominant hand, draw a picture of yourself in the center of the page. In the drawing, surround yourself with all of your passions. Draw symbols or images for each of the things that you are the most passionate about.

3. On a new page, with your dominant hand, write your observations of what you see in the picture.

   • Which things were the closest to you?
   • Which were the farthest away?

- Which passion was drawn the largest and which was the smallest?
- Is there any significance in how the items were placed on the page in relation to each other?

4. Review your list and your picture and ask yourself if there are any individuals or groups who share your passions. Are there any ways you can join with others who are fueled by the same passion?

My Greatest Passion is risk/speed.
Flying, cars, skiing, drag race/legal,
motorcycles — anything fast, and my kids.

I love risk. All kinds. I like speed. My favorite passion is flying. But my children are my greatest passion. . .

When I fly, the best feeling is in the take-off (takeoff and landing are the two most dangerous times when flying). You're cleared for takeoff and the thrill takes over. . .

Planes, cars, cycles—all that is mechanical-based speed and thrill—are my passions.

When you raise children there is no way to "turn right." Sometimes, there is no right. It is truly high risk. You get no training. It is really flying by the seat of your pants. You've got to make your best judgment and judgment is hard to teach. Sometimes you just can't teach it. Like with kids, you can get them educated but how do you teach them judgment?

My passion was and is to teach my kids
two things about judgment. Understand that
a disagreement is just that. You don't have
to destroy a relationship or keep from
having them because you "disagree."
Realize that there are always two sides to
every story. Don't judge. Have an open
mind. Hear the other side.

Kids aren't mechanical. You don't get a
second chance to raise them.

Motorcycles are in the past; my kids are
my passion now. I am a loner, not a joiner. I
share my passions with those closest to me.

Ordinary Places

We find talent in ordinary places and in everyday activities. There
are hundreds of tasks we perform in our daily lives that contain
buried, unrecognized talent. Sometimes others see our abilities more
than we do because we take them for granted. A man who enjoys
cooking gourmet meals for his family may not think of his culinary
activities as a talent. He enjoys it and does it as part of his life's
routine. Making an "art form" out of an ordinary task is often a sign

of innate abilities. Talent takes a job, usually seen as necessary, and elevates it into something worthy of special attention and enjoyment. Such routine activities as dressing, cooking, reading bedtime stories to children, paying the bills, organizing the closets, gardening, or walking the dog often harbor buried treasures of unrecognized talent.

> Mary, a young housewife with two children, found herself divorced and in need of a job. To prepare for finding work, she elected to write down everything she did from one end of the day to the other. In assessing the list, she discovered she was able to name her talents. As a housewife and mother of two young children, Mary was an organizer, financial manager and negotiator. She was artistic as well as a wonderful storyteller and friend to her children. Mary decided to combine these talents. Much to her surprise, she found that she was qualified to fill the administrative needs of a small toy company. Ten years later, she became an executive in a major firm that manufactures educational books, tapes and toys for children. This talented woman looked to her "ordinary, everyday" tasks to identify her capabilities.

Mary's unique blend of creative and bottom-line business talent translated into a successful and personally fulfilling career. By weaving her varied experience into a specialty, she brought together seemingly unrelated skills that rarely appear in one person. Mary has been described by her employers and co-workers alike as being absolutely indispensable. She has become an essential bridge between the creative division and the financial and marketing departments of her company.

Right Under My Nose (Part 1)

MATERIALS: Talent Journal and felt pens

1. Look back into your past and recall any daily living skills that you reshaped into a marketable talent or applied to problem-solving in some other area of your life (community service, church, club, etc.).

   • What skill did you transfer over?
   • How did you capitalize on a skill you were already using on a daily basis?
   • Does your own history of recycling "ordinary skills" into other areas of your life give you any new ideas about how you can do this in your life today?

2. Write about it in your journal.

At 16 years old I bought my first car, a 1969 VW Beetle. It had many problems, to put it mildly. At first it was in the shop every month. I was in high school and didn't have much money, so I realized that I couldn't keep shelling out for repairs. I started fixing the simple things myself, with a little advice from *The Complete Idiot's Guide to VW Repair*, our family mechanic and my dad. I started changing the oil and doing the regular maintenance. People were always surprised because they didn't expect a teenage girl to be the least bit interested in repairing or maintaining a car.

It turned out to be a lot of fun, as well as super economical. I even ended up taking Automotive Service Technology in college and became a mechanic for five years. It all started with that old broken down VW. It was a real pain at first, but it sure forced some talents of mine to show up out of sheer necessity.

Right Under My Nose (Part 2)

MATERIALS: Talent Journal and felt pens

1. On a new page, make a list of your abilities and skills.

2. Select one of the abilities from your list of abilities and skills. Ask yourself, "How can I get paid for this skill?" With your non-dominant hand, write down all the ways you could possibly get paid to use each ability. Don't ponder or analyze, just write the first ideas that come.

Skill: Presentation of food
How can I get paid for this skill?
Write a book
Take pictures of food
Prepare food for others
Do demonstrations
Open a lemonade stand
Write a newspaper column
Start my own magazine

Frustrations

Oftentimes feelings of frustration force hidden talent to come to the surface. Many psychologists agree that all emotions are rooted in joy, love, hurt and fear. Emotions that come out of hurt and fear, such as anger, frustration and sadness, are usually labeled "negative" because they often make us feel uncomfortable. However, these so-called negative emotions can actually catalyze the expression of our deepest talents. Like our passions, emotions can be a powerful source of fuel that sets us into action.

One example is the case of Norma, an interior designer who worked with Peggy. Norma discovered that what she thought of as negative emotions could be a powerful catalyst for change. As Peggy remembers:

> When Norma consulted with me, she said that she was jealous of architects. They had more control. They were the boss. She and the other workers were often treated by them in a patronizing or rude manner. She felt as if she was at the mercy of the architects' poor designs and arrogant attitudes. Burdened by her resentment toward them, she decided to seek my help in reassessing her career.

> In exploring Norma's feelings of jealousy and resentment, I helped her become aware that she needed to focus on her own talents. We found that she had a history as a talented builder and that she really wanted to be an architect. With additional schooling, she knew she could accomplish this. There were few women in architecture, so Norma knew that she would have to create her own career path.

> With the help of a female architect who was happy to serve as Norma's mentor and cheering squad, Norma achieved her goal and became an architect. She is now a role model for young women coming into the profession. What is more important, she recognized that the shortcomings she found in others were nothing more than an invitation to realize a talent hidden within herself.

From Frustration to Satisfaction

MATERIALS: Talent Journal and felt pens

1. Look back in your life and see if there was ever a time when something bothered you so much that instead of complaining about it, you took action.

2. With your dominant hand, write about what bothered you.

   • Was it a person, a behavior or a situation that you found frustrating?
   • Why did you feel frustrated?
   • What did you do about it?
   • How did you feel after you took action?
   • Write about the talent or ability that expressed itself in the process of acting instead of complaining.

Years ago I was told by my husband to shop for our next new car. I did, comparing & researching & test-driving until I knew the one. My husband listened to my reasons &

said to go buy it. I went to the dealership where the salesman had been so anxious to please & explain & sell—identified <u>the</u> one and said we wanted to buy it. The salesman graciously recorded my answers on the paperwork, then sat back and said, "When can your husband come in to sign this?" Even though I had a solid credit record, he wouldn't sell me a car because I didn't have a job.

Angry at being treated like a child (or less), I got a job, worked full-time & got a degree while working—and in five short years. Then I got a much better job and was able to buy my own car. I took action because of what bothered me—his arrogant attitude, his devaluing me as a person, a responsible, tax-paying citizen. I showed myself and the world I am intelligent, responsible, capable of playing & winning their games while abiding by their rules.

Crisis

Crisis can force our natural talents to the surface. When crisis strikes, we often have to make some big decisions. The energy compressed by frustration and tension is ready to be released and seeks a way to express itself. Crisis can be a very special opportunity that draws upon our innate abilities to find creative solutions. One saying we've heard that reflects this is, "Every disappointment is a blessing in disguise." Another one is, "For every door that closes, another one opens up." Lucia remembers this lesson well.

> In 1947, the film industry began slowing down. My father was laid off from MGM Studios just as his editing career was really taking off. It was a crushing blow for him and a financial disaster for our family. After working outside the movie industry for about a year, he got some freelance work on independent films. Then the lucky break of his life came along. He was hired to be the film editor on *The Lone Ranger*, the first filmed series for television. Getting in on the ground floor of this new industry enabled him to rise quickly and become a supervising editor. He had steady work in television for years, until he decided to retire.

Turning Crisis into Opportunity (Part 1)

MATERIALS: Talent Journal and felt pens

1. Think back in your life and recall the major crises that you have experienced (accidents, illness, divorce, death in the family, relocation, job loss, etc.).

2. On your journal page, with your dominant hand, create two columns. Column one is

labeled **crisis** and column two is labeled **opportunity.**

3. In column one, with your dominant hand, list the crises in your life in chronological order.

4. Next to each item in column two, with your non-dominant hand, write down what opportunity presented itself from this crisis.

Turning Crisis into Opportunity (Part 2)

MATERIALS: Talent Journal and felt pens

1. Are you facing a crisis in your life at this time? With your non-dominant hand, draw a picture of it.

   • What shape is the crisis?
   • What color is it?
   • Give the crisis a name and write it on your picture.

2. If the crisis in your drawing could speak, what would it say? Interview it by writing a conversation with it. Use your dominant hand to write the questions, and your non-dominant hand to write the answers from the crisis. Ask the crisis:

   • Why are you here?
   • What do you want from me?
   • What are you here to give me?

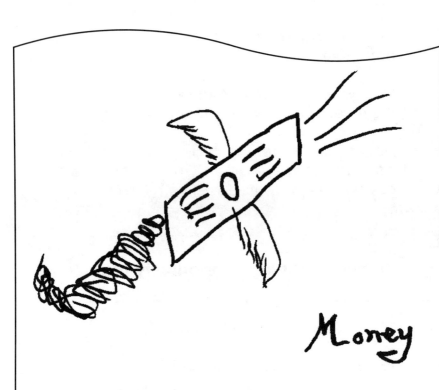

Money

What is the name of your crisis at hand?

The nature of my crisis is money. Money flying out the window. I could have also drawn a picture of a deep well with pictures of lots of money pouring into the deep well and me just standing there shocked that I don't have any. In fact, it barely stopped to touch me. Just went right through.

Transitions

Transitions can be frightening times as we pass from one point in life to another. Relocations, job changes, endings of relationships and other shifts in routine are often filled with uncertainty. In facing changes, identifying our talents can facilitate a smoother transition. We get clarity about who we are, what we value and where we want to go. A personal inventory can reveal the areas where we want to change and grow. Regardless of whether or not we are facing big changes, self-inventory is an important survival skill.

Raymond had just celebrated his 60th birthday when he was forcibly retired from his job in an insurance company. He and his co-workers, who were in the same boat, were upset with this unexpected turn of events. His friends decided to retire, but Raymond felt differently. He did not accept the notion that it was time to be "put out to pasture." This highly experienced and dedicated man sat down one day and listed everything he knew about himself and the insurance business. This exercise broadened and bolstered his confidence and gave him a new perception of his possibilities.

Raymond decided to offer his services as a consultant in an advisory capacity. He talked with many young executives and discovered that while they were long on energy and computer smarts, they were short on networking and interpersonal skills. Building on this information, Raymond got some young executives together and offered to coach them. They responded enthusiastically. He had found a market for his talent.

Naming talents that emerge during transitions can open up exciting new directions. We take all of our knowledge and experience with us into every new situation.

I hate where you work! Get out of there.
The people are weird.

I'm looking for a new job. I just haven't
found a better place yet.

I'm glad you're looking for a place that's
better and more fun.

Endings and Beginnings (Part 1)

MATERIALS: Talent Journal and felt pens

1. Once again, think back in your life and recall the major crises that you have experienced (accidents, illness, divorce, death in the family, relocation, job loss, etc.).

2. On your journal page, with your dominant hand, create two columns. Column one is labeled **endings** and column two is labeled **beginnings.**

3. In column one, with your dominant hand, make a list of the important endings in life: graduation, divorce, leaving a job, menopause, etc.

4. In column two, with your non-dominant hand, write down the new beginning that followed from the ending listed in the first column.

Endings	Beginnings
Boyfriend left me	Married high school sweetheart
Got laid off	Found a better job
Fire destroyed house	Built a new and better house
Kids left home and got married	Started traveling

Endings and Beginnings (Part 2)

MATERIALS: Talent Journal and felt pens

1. What is coming to an end at this time in your life? With your non-dominant hand, draw a picture of it.

2. What is just beginning at this time in your life? With your non-dominant hand, draw a picture of it.

3. After you have completed your picture, using your dominant hand, write down your observations.

I have punished myself, dishonoring myself for so very long by smoking. Oh, I punished so many people with every deep inhale and blew all of my troubles with that great long exhale. But the people I punished never felt it. I was only succeeding in punishing myself.

I quit smoking and now I smell as fresh as Spring. I feel so much better about myself. Those people closest to me are so very happy . . . they want me to live and be healthy.

Mapping Your Talent (Part 1)

MATERIALS: Talent Journal and felt pens

Draw a map of your talents, starting in childhood.

1. With your non-dominant hand, draw a road or path that represents your life from birth to the present time.

2. Start at the beginning of the path. Make a chronological map by drawing symbols or images that represent the birth of a particular talent or ability you have.

3. Next to each talent, indicate what age you were when this ability first surfaced.

4. By each symbol or image, write the name of the talent. Use your dominant hand.

3. Look at your talent map. On a new page, write your impressions, observations and discoveries with your dominant hand.

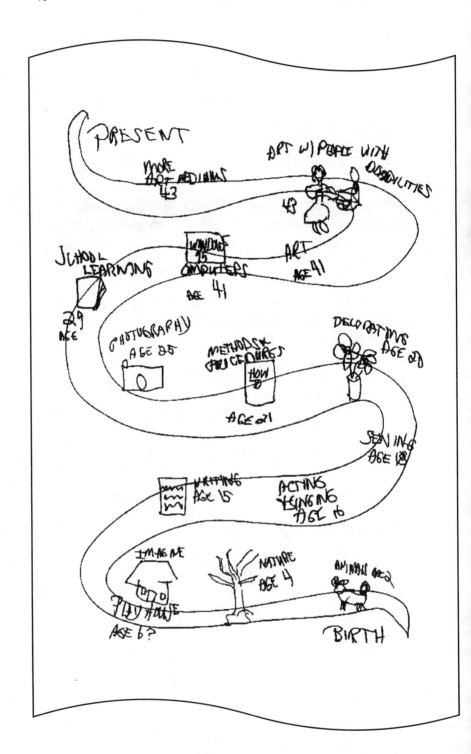

Mapping Your Talent (Part 2)

MATERIALS: Talent Journal and felt pens

1. Choose one talent that is most important to you at this time. With your dominant hand, write a letter of appreciation to that talent as though it were a person. For instance: Dear Organizer, or Dear Salesperson, or Dear Musician, etc.

2. With your non-dominant hand, draw a picture of how that talent would look if it were a person.

3. Using both hands, write out a conversation with this particular talent. With your dominant hand, ask this talent (as if it were a person) any question you wish. With your non-dominant hand, let the talent answer. Some suggested questions are:
   - How can I honor you and help you grow?
   - What blocks you from fully expressing in my life?
   - How do you want to express in my life?
   - How can you help me receive money or support for expressing you in my life?

Dear Artist,

This is a letter of appreciation. Thank you for being in my life. You know I live just for you. You are my reason for living. It is through you that I know myself and I know God. My life would indeed be very dark without you.

Love, Me

Artist, tell me: how can I honor you and help you grow?

Keep doing what you are doing. Draw every day. You find God that way. You must draw on your skills.

What blocks you from fully expressing?

You put others before me. You just can't do that. I am too important. I know you are conscientious and mean well, but I am what you need.

How do you want to express in my life?

Good question. Maybe neither of us knows. Externalize what's inside you — tap further down — keep painting and drawing. You must. You are the artist — YOU HAVE CHOICE. Go deeper.

How can you help me receive money or support for expressing you in my life?

If you go deeper, I will help you. I promise.

CHAPTER TWO

ACCEPTING TALENT

Once found and named, talent needs to be accepted. These are the first building blocks to fully developing our talent. This simply means that a particular talent is acknowledged as a part of us that we value and embrace. All of the people we described in the first chapter succeeded not only because they named their talent, but because they accepted it as well.

Non-Acceptance of Talent

Signs of Non-Acceptance

Unaccepted talent has a way of making itself known to us. It sends up red flags in our everyday lives. Like neglected children, our unexpressed talents cry out for love and attention. Most of us are unaware that our unaccepted talent is speaking to us. How does talent let us know that it's trying to get out? Through our emotions, behavior, body and relationships. The following are some indications of unrecognized talents:

Emotional signs:

- fear
- frustration
- depression
- boredom
- anger and resentment
- jealousy and envy

Behavioral clues:

- non-productivity
- passivity
- procrastination
- avoidance
- indecisiveness

Physical symptoms:

- stress
- low energy
- chronic illness
- accident proneness
- headaches
- indigestion
- constipation

There is a common thread to all of these conditions. They are all associated with lack of forward movement. If all or many of these signs, clues or symptoms ring true for you, it may be time to take notice.

Relationship conflicts also tend to surface as a result of not accepting our talents. Some telltale signs of blocked talent are chronic feelings of envy, jealousy, resentment and criticism of others. If we don't know who we are and how we behave, we can't take the right action, nor will we be in harmony with others. Sometimes this plays itself out as envy or jealousy cloaked in criticism toward others who are successfully expressing their talents. This is especially true if a person's talent is the same or similar to the talent we are neglecting.

Blocks to Accepting Talent

The biggest barrier to accepting our talent is destructive criticism. Talent needs a safe, fertile ground in which to grow. It needs to be encouraged and nurtured. Talent springs forth from our Creative Child self. This part of us knows how to play, explore the unknown, and be open to new ideas and experiences. The Child self is also fragile and sensitive to harsh treatment. Destructive criticism throws a wet blanket on creativity. It can severely hamper the acceptance of our innate gifts.

The Inner Critic

Many of us perpetuate negative self-talk about talents that we don't accept. Self-criticism can seriously injure potential talent that wants to be expressed. This negative self-talk comes in a variety of forms. Sometimes we hear it in our own voice. It says things like: *I don't really have it. I'm not good enough. It won't work. I'll fail. I'll make mistakes and look foolish. I can't make a living with my talent.*

Often inner criticism sounds like a parent or some authority figure from our past. Frequently it compares us to others and we always come out the loser. It will say things like: *You're no Rembrandt. Why not just give up on art? Hemingway was a writer; you're not. Your brother is the businessman in the family; you'll never be as good as he is.*

At other times, we may project this negative message onto others in the form of imagined external criticism. We anticipate that others will ridicule us or put us down before we even attempt to develop our talent. The fact is that we haven't even given others a chance to react at all. We've erected the barrier of fear born out of our own negative self-talk.

Fortunately, talent waits patiently behind our fear and self-doubt. As it waits, it sends up one message after another, like smoke signals emanating from a distant unseen fire. Emotional signs, behavioral clues, physical symptoms and relationship conflicts can bring our attention to the underlying fear that blocks our talent's expression. To deal with the fear, we must acknowledge what is causing our fear: the Inner Critic. We need to uncover it, let it have its say and then do what we really want to do. The object is to move beyond the fear so that our abilities can be developed.

Growth is often the close companion of risk. Risk and fear go hand in hand. This is both natural and normal. If something is easy, there is no fear or risk. No risk, no growth. When fear paralyzes us, stops us dead in our tracks, we're trapped. When negative self-talk robs us of our enthusiasm for our dreams, we're suffering from the classic creative block. You don't have to be an artist to have a creative block. In one of Lucia's career counseling sessions, her client, Joanna, spoke of her many aborted attempts to start a small retail dress shop. Joanna wanted very much to create something new. She had a strong vision but was blocked.

I asked Joanna to tell me exactly what happened inside when she tried to actually work on this project.

"Every time I start actually working on the business plan or anything concrete that might take me closer to my goal, I hear this voice in my head," Joanna complained. "It nags and predicts doom until I get a splitting headache. It happens every time," she concluded grimly.

I suggested a little experiment. "Would you be willing to stand up over there and deliver the speech you keep hearing in your head when you work on this business project?" Joanna laughed nervously, but agreed to go ahead. When she got up, I coached her. "Are you the voice in Joanna's head that gives her a headache?" When she nodded, I continued. "What do you think of Joanna's business ideas? Say anything you want. You've got the floor."

Joanna, speaking for her Inner Critic, said, "This is the stupidest idea I ever heard of. She's living in fantasy land. She's got a good job. What she needs to do is just stay where she is. Her boss likes her. Why can't she just work for him like everybody else, collect a paycheck and be satisfied with that?" As the Critic spoke, Joanna became stiffer and stiffer, her face wrinkled up and she actually looked years older. When Joanna was through role-playing, she sat down and let out a big sigh. "My God. You just met MY MOTHER. That's how she talks and that's the kind of stuff she says. No wonder I get headaches."

"Look, Joanna," I said, "from what you've already told me about your work history and your current job, you *are* a good businesswoman. But YOU have to believe it. Your Inner

Critic has been stronger than the truth and it has been stronger than the feedback of experienced business professionals who believe in you."

Joanna wanted to know how she could believe in herself. I responded, "By accepting that you are a *talented business-woman*, Joanna. By learning to tell the truth about yourself, *to yourself* and to others. But FIRST you'll need to deal with that voice in your head that drowns out your talent and negates who you really are."

Joanna's other negative self-talk included, "I'm afraid that if I open a dress shop, customers will not come." Behind this fear, we unearthed a veritable Greek chorus of anonymous "customers" in her head saying things like: "Oh, what stupid-looking stuff. These prices are too high. I can't find anything I like here. I'm just looking." Before she knew it, Joanna had driven herself into bankruptcy on a business that hadn't even opened. She did it all in her own imagination with self-critical chatter.

When Joanna followed up with journal work designed to expose and counteract the Inner and Outer Critics, she worked up the confidence to open her own shop. By teaming up with an investor, she put her talent for marketing and sales to work. Her business has been a huge success.

> **"Nobody can do anything to me**
> **that I'm not already doing to myself."**
>
> **Eleanor Roosevelt**

The question remains: Where does the Inner Critic come from? We learned it growing up. It is rooted in our survival abilities, our Protective Self. This is the part of us that knows the laws and the rules and abides by them. Growing up, we all learned rules for behavior, what was acceptable and what was not. "Wash your hands before coming to the table. Don't leave your roller skates on the front porch for someone to trip over. Finish your class assignment or you can't go out for recess."

Some of our actions earned praise or rewards. "Oh, what a beautiful bouquet. You remembered my birthday. Aren't you sweet." Other actions we took (or didn't take) simply averted punishment. We did our homework because we didn't want to fail at school or be subjected to our parents' wrath. Still other behavior brought dire consequences. "That's it. You're grounded for a week. Now you're going to get a whipping. No allowance for a month."

As young children, totally dependent on adults and society, we needed to play by the rules to survive. We still do. There's nothing wrong with limits and regulations as long as they are appropriate for the time and place. Life would be totally chaotic without commonly held laws and guidelines for behavior. As adults, when we break big enough rules, we get arrested, lose our jobs, destroy our marriages or other relationships. Even if we don't agree with certain rules, we get along in life by paying attention to the laws and to those who enforce them.

The Inner Critic perpetuates self-doubt by imitating past authority figures who told us we were no good. It fills us with fear and shame in the deepest part of our being. It continues to hypnotize us with negative self-talk. Our Inner Critic is dedicated to keeping us on the straight and narrow path; but whose straight and narrow path is it? Our mother's or father's? Our fifth-grade teacher's, whose name we can't even remember? The boss's at our very first job? Without realizing it, we grow into adulthood with all these other voices internalized in our minds, shaping our lives. By confronting those critical voices in our heads, it is possible to disempower them.

Rules About Roles

As children, we learned many rules about roles that were acceptable and roles that were out of bounds. These rules reflected the beliefs and prejudices of authority figures: our parents, teachers and other opinion shapers. Some commonly held prejudices about career roles are:

> "There are no women composers, mechanics, astronauts, presidents, etc.; so it's not a viable choice for a female."

> "Male artists, poets, hairdressers are all gay, so it's not okay for a boy or man to pursue such a career."

> "Without an advanced degree you can't succeed."

> "You're too old to (start a new career, change jobs, go back to school, start a new hobby, open a new business)."

> "You're not smart enough, well-read enough, creative enough, or attractive enough to (go to medical school, become a writer, be a designer, become an actress)."

Ask yourself if the talent you want to develop was considered off-limits or inappropriate by your family, teachers, peers, etc. Ask yourself if you simply never saw any role models who were expressing that particular gift. Did you conclude early on that developing a particular interest was just an impractical fantasy? The Inner Critic is much like the emperor in the fairy tale, *The Emperor's New Clothes*. As long as you believe what the Critic says, it will run your life. So long as your Critic is a dictatorial king (or queen), your talent will be an orphan out on the fringes of our lives. Once you pull the covers off the Critic's game, the jig is up.

Confronting the Inner Critic

MATERIALS: Talent Journal and felt pens

1. Turn to a double-page spread. On the left-hand page, with your dominant hand, draw a picture of the Inner Critic who puts your talent down. This is the face behind the voice in your head that says you have no talent, will never succeed and should forget your heart's desires.

2. In your picture, with your dominant hand, create word balloons around the Critic containing the statements it makes that feel like put-downs.

3. On another page, with your non-dominant hand, write down the names of all the people in your life (living or dead) who helped shape your negative self-talk. It may have been your nagging father, your witchy third-grade teacher, your hyper-critical college professor, etc.

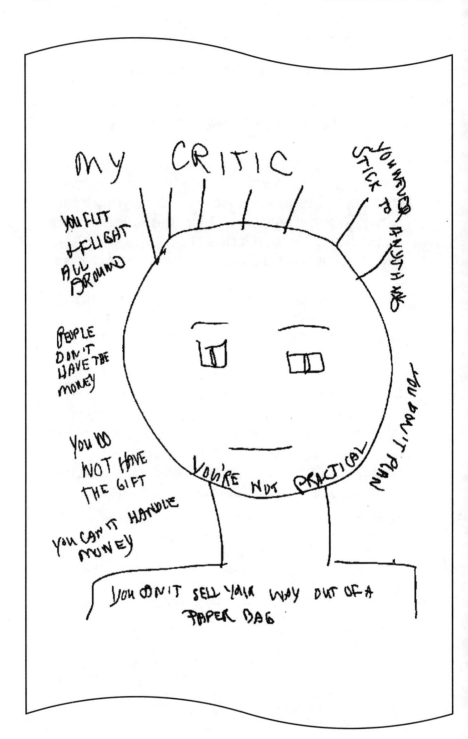

The Outer Critic

In addition to our Inner Critic, there may be people in our lives who discourage us from following our heart and our gifts. For whatever reason, they believe we are on the wrong track when we follow our talent instead of their advice. One such person was Gary, a young sculptor with a very strong background in anatomy.

Gary showed artistic talent at an early age. However, his parents wanted him to go to medical school and were willing to pay for it. They did not want to pay for an education in art. Gary insisted on going to art school and was able to get a student loan. During his third year, he had a sculpture teacher who was exceptionally critical. His motto was: Criticism will toughen you up for dealing with the "real world."

After being "toughened" for a couple of semesters, Gary began to cave in. He heard the negative voice of his instructor tearing down his work before even starting to sculpt. Gary quit the class after being told he didn't have enough talent in his hands to putty a wall, let alone sculpt a figure.

His parents were glad that their son had been "told the truth" and that he had come to his senses. He enrolled in medical school with their blessing and financial support.

Gary went through medical school half-heartedly. Classes in anatomy and kinesiology brightened his day and he excelled in them. Six months before graduation, the young man saw a newspaper ad for a sculptor at a toy company. It occurred to him that he should try one more time, no matter what his parents or teachers thought. He applied, interviewed, got the job and never went back to medical school.

The first time he picked up a piece of clay at his new job, Gary heard the sculpture teacher's voice telling him he had no talent. He decided to keep sculpting anyway. Happiness came from sculpting. Gary kept sculpting until he got beyond his inner criticism and was able to do his job.

It's never too late to give talent a second chance. Gary was persistent and defeated his negative self-talk. The following activity can help you do the same if your Inner Critic is blocking your heart's desire.

Telling It Like It Is (Part 1)

MATERIALS: Talent Journal and felt pens

Using your non-dominant hand, write a letter to the Inner Critic that's in your head 24 hours a day, every day of the year. Tell the Critic about the talent you are going to cultivate; tell the Critic how you feel about its treatment of you and your talent. Let the critic know *what you want* and that *you are going to get it.*

Letter To Inner Critic,

Look, we've been together for a long time. Perhaps I can turn your energies into something positive. To my benefit. I don't appreciate your holding me back from making money. We need the money so I can develop my talent. Art supplies are very expensive, and I need a vacation. There are things I need to see and do that cost money (like pomegranates in the spring in San Francisco/California). I WANT TO MAKE MONEY with my art and I AM GOING TO GET IT. So there!

The Artist in Residence

Telling It Like It Is (Part 2)

MATERIALS: Talent Journal and felt pens

With your dominant hand, write a letter to all those who have discouraged you or tried to keep your talent from growing. You can address the letter to them as a group (To the Critics in My Life) or write letters to individuals who have put you down and dampened your dream. Include people who noticeably withheld support when they could have given it. This letter is for your eyes only. It is not to be sent.

Tell the critics exactly how you feel about their negative attitudes, beliefs and behavior. Really let your feelings out. If anger surfaces, allow its full expression in your letter. Use four-letter words if you want. Anything goes. *Remember, this letter is just for your eyes, no holds barred.* Get it out of your system and onto the paper.

Note: If you have trouble getting to your feelings, try writing this letter with your non-dominant hand. This method helps express feelings (a right-brain function) and enables us to let out anger that is buried under our low energy, depression, frustration and lack of enthusiasm.

Dear Critics in My Life,

You guys have colluded all these years by saying nothing. What am I supposed to think? I go on—keep trying to get it right—to please you. I want to hear: "You're wonderful! What you do is fabulous! No one in the world can do this like you!" But no, you're silent. Well, I am going to change that. You'll see!

The Artist

When you feel particularly discouraged or depressed, write one of these letters. Your emotional self (your Inner Child) is probably still angry about being criticized over the years by all the Critics in your life. It's time to let that Child *have* its real feelings and *let them out* in a safe place.

Buried underneath the depression and lack of motivation, you may find some very powerful feelings that have life, vitality and much energy. Remember, anger is hot. (Think of common phrases like: "He was burned up. She was hot under the collar. His face was beet-red with rage.") Anger is alive. Anger is active. It can fuel creative action. It can help you reclaim your birthright: your innate talent. It can go a long way toward helping you accept your talent.

The Critic Turned Inside Out

If we don't confront the Inner Critic or deal with our feelings about destructive criticism from others, our buried anger can backfire like a volcano when we least expect it. That's why it is so important to become aware of our anger about being put down. If we don't deal with it, that anger can spill out destructively on others and damage our relationships. One case in point is Molly, a young woman with whom Peggy worked.

Molly had an overwhelming desire to be a trainer for her company. She was technically qualified for the position, but had stage fright and blocked herself from developing presentation skills. When speaking to a group she would hear her negative self-talk and freeze with fear. Her Inner Critic (a real perfectionist) would tell her she wasn't doing a good enough job. She thought she was a failure.

Molly had compared herself with those she saw doing training sessions and felt that their abilities far surpassed hers. Molly's Inner Critic gave her such bad reviews that she didn't even attempt to interview for the position of trainer. However, she decided that her technical expertise would qualify her as a program developer. In this position, she could at least write material for the training sessions. Molly applied and was accepted.

The job required her to work closely with the trainers. She was asked to sit in on the training sessions to help evaluate their use of the materials she wrote. At first, she felt intimidated and rarely made any comments. However, when she was asked to critique the trainers, no one seemed to please her. She had a reputation for being very critical of the trainers.

Molly decided to work with me after her manager had told her that none of the trainers liked working with her. They said they would only teach her material if she were not part of the critiquing process. The manager saw this as a serious performance problem, but Molly couldn't understand why everyone was upset. She just wanted the material to be presented as well as possible. Oblivious to her own negative self-talk, she was unaware of the unreasonable demands her Inner Critic was making on others.

When she came to me for career counseling, I pointed out that hyper-critical attitudes are often signals indicating that a talent is being frustrated. We were able to move right to the difficulty. The truth was that Molly wanted to present the material she wrote. Her desire was blocked by her inability to accept that she could become a presenter. Also, the envy and jealousy she admittedly harbored toward the presenters were symptoms of blocked talent.

We put a plan together for Molly. She signed up for a series of presentation classes and asked the instructors to give her objective feedback. While she was taking these classes, Molly agreed to let the trainers teach her material without her having to evaluate them.

Molly's presentation instructors were very encouraging and told her that with sufficient practice she could become an excellent presenter. The image she had of herself did not match up with the observations of her experienced instructors. As she cultivated her own talent, she realized how critical she was of herself and how excessively critical she had been with the trainers. Eventually, Molly was able to forgive herself, apologize to the trainers and move ahead.

As she gained confidence in her talent and skills, Molly began talking to her manager about her interest in a training position. When the opportunity arose, she interviewed and got the job. Furthermore, her new manager was very open to letting Molly write her own course material. She was the only trainer in the company allowed to do this.

Perfectionism is another disguise that the Inner Critic wears. Nothing is ever good enough for the perfectionist. Whatever we do, we just don't measure up. Setting high standards and honoring quality is one thing, but perfectionism-run-rampant can be a killer of talent. This is especially true when perfectionism strikes at the beginning steps of talent development. We must make mistakes to learn; we will feel awkward as we develop new skills. The perfectionist has no tolerance for such discomfort. The impatient perfectionist wants perfection *now*. These are impossible expectations. They strangle the voice of emerging abilities and throw us back into a hole of self-doubt and depression.

The best way to counteract the lies your Inner Critic tells you about your talent is to **tell the truth about your talent. Feed yourself positive self-talk.**

Nothing But the Truth (Part 1)

MATERIALS: Talent Journal and felt pens

1. With your dominant hand, draw a picture of your "talent self." Draw yourself engaged in expressing those abilities that you want to cultivate. If it's the Inner Writer, show yourself busily developing writing skills, producing a body of work, etc. If it's the Inner Scientist, show yourself at work in the lab or wherever else. This is your totally capable self putting your talent to work.

2. With your dominant hand, draw dialog balloons around your "talent self" in which you speak the truth. Project yourself into the future. You are already expressing your talent, so write *in the present tense.*

At first, affirmations may sound phony to you, especially if you have spent many years believing your Critic's negative chatter. When the "new" voice says, "I'm a really good administrator," the old voice may pop out and tell you, "You're a liar, a fake, an actor who is just pretending." Watch for character assassination (a specialty of the Inner Critic, who doesn't know the meaning of the word constructive).

Be patient and tenacious. It may take a bit of time to get used to positive reinforcement. If the battle gets hot and heavy between your new truth-telling talent voice and the old naggy negative voice, just let them duke it out for a while.

Nothing But the Truth (Part 2)

MATERIALS: Talent Journal and felt pens

1. With your dominant hand, create two columns with the following headings:

   Talent's Truth   **Critic's Opinion**

2. In column one, **Talent's Truth**, with your non-dominant hand, write out a true statement about your talent.

3. In column two, **Critic's Opinion**, with your dominant hand, write out the critic's reaction to your positive, true statement.

4. With your non-dominant hand, repeat your true statement in column one, **Talent's Truth**. With your dominant hand, write the critic's opinion in column two, **Critic's Opinion**.

5. Continue alternating back and forth until you feel an inner conviction about your talent's truth. This may take awhile. You may need to do it more than once, but it will be well worth the effort.

TALENT'S TRUTH	CRITIC'S OPINION
My work is sensitive and full of meaning and truth. For this reason, people will buy it.	Yes, you are sensitive, but you don't have the gift. You can't even design.
My work is sensitive and full of meaning and truth. For this reason, people will buy it.	Even if it is truthful, it isn't beautiful. It is not skillful. You are an amateur.
My work is sensitive and full of meaning and truth. For this reason, people will buy it.	There are much better pieces around they will buy. They will not buy yours.

My work is sensitive
and full of meaning
and truth.
For this reason,
people will buy it.

It just isn't worth
money.
It's nice for you
—you feel good
you can do it—
but it is for you.

You can't even draw
or paint. HA!
You can't even mix
colors in print-
making.
You poor slob!

Hey, who are you
calling a slob?
I am the
resident
artist!

SELF-PERCEPTION AND FEAR

Sometimes our Inner Critic appears to support us. It can seduce us into sticking to what we know because it really doesn't want us to try anything new. When this happens, we identify ourselves with a single, dominant talent and exclude the existence of other talents. We tell ourselves that we would be bored or unhappy doing anything else and that it would be foolish to try. The longer we stay with a given expertise, the harder it is to accept any other talents we may have. Finding success in a single talent can convince us that we cannot or should not do anything else. We become trapped by our expertise. The truth is that we don't want to move out of our comfort zone. Being "an expert" is very ego-gratifying, but if we can't be life-long learners, we stagnate. With stagnation comes boredom. In not accepting our multi-talented nature, we plant the seeds of inflexibility and hamper our ability to adapt and survive.

In working with companies who are downsizing, we have seen many men and women who were trapped by their own expertise. Peggy recalls one case:

> Gus was an engineer in a computer manufacturing firm. He had developed a level of expertise in his company that was legendary. During the downsizing of the company, he was convinced that his services would be retained at any cost to the company. He was sure he would be needed to develop the new product that would lead his company out of its current financial dilemma. He did not count on the company stopping all development in his area. When this happened, it came as a shock to Gus. He was unprepared.
>
> The company appreciated his talent and offered him a position in another division. He would still be doing research and development, but would have to redirect his talent and energy in another field. Gus felt trapped. He thought he wouldn't be happy doing anything else. He wouldn't ever be as good working in another area. What could he do? He assumed that his age and salary level would prevent him

from taking his expertise to another company. Gus didn't want to retire. With nothing to look forward to, he thought he would die of boredom. Gus narrowed his self-perception, limited his options and became fearful. He had every reason to feel trapped. He was.

We began working together, identifying all the achievements of his career. Before he had become specialized, Gus had been far more accepting of his other abilities. Getting him to recall and acknowledge his many gifts was the first step in helping him see beyond his primary skill. Being an engineer, he saw himself as a problem-solver. It turned out that he had excellent research and communication skills, which he hadn't acknowledged. With diligence, he was able to broaden his self-perception, accept his talents and put them to work in a new context.

Like Gus, many of us fall into a trap when we fail to accept our multi-talented nature. However, the need to survive might come along and give us a whack on the side of the head. If we want to work or stay in business, we may have to expand and diversify. This is especially true in today's ever-changing business climate. By seeking Peggy's support and being willing to change his self-definition, Gus was able to move into a new career direction. This change revitalized him and enriched his life immeasurably.

SUPPORT FOR TALENT:
STRENGTH IN NUMBERS

Support is a key element in moving beyond our negative self-talk. Getting help from others to break old perceptions of who we are and what we are capable of doing can make all the difference in the world. A well-known example of the power of support is the 12-Step program, Alcoholics Anonymous. AA has been a pioneer in the support movement. Treatment for alcoholics had been notoriously unsuccessful using a medical model. The self-help group model of treatment gave rise to a greater success rate. In fact, most treatment centers now have 12-Step meetings or similar approaches built into their programs.

Success Teams, as developed by Barbara Sher, author of *Wishcraft*, are also ideal settings for nurturing dreams and cultivating new behaviors. Through group encouragement in a safe, non-judgmental atmosphere, participants get support for telling the truth about their dreams.

We recommend support groups if you are serious about hurdling the obstacles to realizing your talent. If you can't find a support group in your area (or can't afford career counseling), take a grassroots approach and start your own support group.

> Tyrone, a young building contractor, had developed a friendship with two sisters, Sylvia and Maria, who were doing freelance work in interactive multimedia. They all felt the need for career support and decided to have luncheon meetings every week. At their first get-together they devised an assignment. Each member would list his or her long- and short-term goals.
>
> At the next meeting, they shared their goals as well as their fears, frustrations and progress. They supported each other through the difficulties and celebrated their successes. The group found that writing and continually reading, updating and analyzing their goals helped them to stay focused on their dreams.
>
> After six months, each member of the group had accomplished his or her short-term goals. This gave them confidence to face their long-term goals. They all agreed that this group approach helped them get more work accomplished, with less stress. As a result of these focused meetings and group support, each member's career has taken a dramatic leap forward.

Positive group energy can make a huge difference if you are trying to break the hypnotic spell of the Inner Critic. Such support can also be an opportunity for locating resources and information needed to develop talent. Chapter seven contains guidelines on how to start and conduct a support group. Sources for materials, classes, professional services, books and computer software are often shared in these sessions. Mutual moral support among group members is the most valuable benefit.

BOUNDARIES AND LIMITS ON CRITICISM

As we learn to get support for our talent, it is equally important to protect ourselves from the criticism of others. Once we learn how to deal with our Inner Critic, handling criticism from others is much easier. The following activity helps you identify those who help and those who hinder you in your talent development.

Eliminate the Negative

MATERIALS: Talent Journal and felt pens

1. With your dominant hand, make a list titled: **Critics.** Write down the names of all those who discourage you from following your heart, from being your true self.

2. After each person's name, with your dominant hand, specify how that person contributes to your negative self-image.

3. With your dominant hand, make another list titled: **Supporters.** This time, write down the

names of the people you feel safe sharing your dream with. These are the people who encourage you and provide support in whatever way they can.

4. After each person's name, with your dominant hand, write down specifically how each of these people helps you identify and develop your talents and abilities.

SUPPORTERS

Dain supports me financially. He thinks I should pursue the cards.

Carol & Mary Lou always say thank you for my cards & that they liked them.

Mary has said: "You should work with kids."

Lu thinks I am creative. Supports my going ahead with creative endeavors as an artist.

While you're learning the truth about your talent, it is important to stop feeding yourself lies. That includes lies coming from outside. Get in the habit of observing when and if others put your talent or your dreams down. If you catch people in the act of trampling your treasures, you can do something about it. If you care about the relationship, tell the person how you feel about his or her negative statement. Here are some examples:

> "It's not helpful to me when you laugh at the mention of my changing careers or going back to school or developing this new skill."

> "I need support while following my dream. If you can't offer me any encouragement, then please don't make any comments."

You may feel nervous about asking for help. Prepare yourself by writing your statements out in your journal. In some cases, you may have to spend less time with certain friends or associates. If a relationship is counter-productive for your own growth, you may need to discontinue that relationship. Give yourself the space to get your self-esteem and career on track. If some people simply cannot support your wishes and needs (for whatever reason), then they do not have your best interest at heart, no matter what they say. Beware of those who say they know what's best for you. No one has the right to run your life. You have to live with yourself and the decisions you make. Nobody else can walk in your shoes or know what action you should take.

Learning to declare what you want and don't want in your life is a crucial step in furthering your talent. We call it "declaration" because it has to be said out loud to others. After all, others won't know what you want (or don't want) unless you tell them. The next activity will help you learn to declare yourself. It will also help you shield yourself from the criticism, envy or resentment of others who (for whatever reason) don't want you to develop your talent.

Finding Support and Setting Boundaries

MATERIALS: Talent Journal and felt pens

1   Read the list titled **Supporters** that you made in
    the last activity, **Eliminate the Negative.** With
    your dominant hand, write down what you can
    do to build up your support team. Who can
    you ask for support? Specifically, how do you
    want people to support you in strengthening
    your self-confidence and nurturing your talent?

2. Read the list titled **Critics** that you made in the
    last activity, **Eliminate the Negative**. Then ask
    yourself what you can do about the nay-sayers
    who put you down or in some way throw a wet
    blanket on your enthusiasm and faith. Write
    down what you intend to do about each one
    of these non-supportive people in your life. In
    some cases you may need to confront the
    person and set clear boundaries to protect
    yourself and your talent. You can prepare for
    this by doing the letter writing exercise earlier in
    this chapter.

ACCEPTING YOUR TALENT, EMBRACING A NEW SELF

Once you learn how to deal with criticism, you can pursue your
heart's desire. How do you do this? Create your life, the way artists
and designers create anything tangible. Make your vision into
physical reality.

Uncovering and acknowledging a talent that is trying to surface in your life means embracing a newly discovered part of yourself. Think of it as a role, if you like. Give your talent a personality. Get in touch with your Inner Dancer or Inner Scientist or Inner Business Owner or whatever talent it is that wants to see the light of day.

Artists and designers usually begin the process of creating new buildings, objects or anything else by first visualizing with the mind's eye, then transferring their mental picture into some material form. Perhaps they start with a sketch on a napkin, a scale model, a diagram or floor plan.

This process can be applied to designing your life and work. The first step is naming your talent. The next step is identifying your talent visually by picturing it on paper. This is your blueprint. This is your way to fully accept the talent that is attempting to reveal itself. The next activity will show you how to go about this magical process of creating a "visual affirmation."

Visioning Your Talent at Work

MATERIALS: Collage supplies

1. Create a visual affirmation by making a photo collage of your Talent Self. First, go through magazines and clip pictures that really grab you. You can also include words and phrases to be used as captions that express your Talent Self picture. Don't try to be rational about this. Just let yourself choose the pictures you like. If your Inner Critic jumps in and tries to control this process, being practical or reasonable or trashing the whole project, just ask it to take a

coffee break. Continue going through the magazine and cutting out pictures, words and captions that speak to you.

2. When you feel you have the pictures and captions you want, begin placing them on your art paper. The idea is to express the life you want to live, the work you want to do, the skills you want to build, the contributions you want to make with your talent. You may be surprised at how perfect certain "found" words or phrases will be in expressing your true desires.

3. When you're ready, begin gluing the photos down on your art paper. Use the same approach you did while selecting the images. Follow your feelings, follow your heart. If your Art Critic starts hammering away about the aesthetic merits of your collage, again just ask it to take a vacation. Continue. This collage is for YOU—not for your Inner Critic and certainly not for any outer Critics, real or imagined.

4. Put your visual affirmation collage up in a place where you can see it often. Keep reinforcing the imagery in your pictures by looking at them and seeing your talented self as a reality. If you wish, create a special place for this collage, a place where you honor your talent.

TALENT WORKOUT

Heart's Desire

Talent expresses through your heart's desire. Each morning, ask yourself:

What is my heart's desire for today?

This can pertain to any aspect of your life: leisure, relationships, home, dining, exercise, hobbies, etc. During the day, ask yourself the same question, perhaps at noon and then again at dinner time. "What is my heart's desire?" should echo in your mind throughout the day.

The purpose of this practice is to develop the habit of consulting your heart. It is one of the best ways we know to get into the habit of listening to your talent. This is especially true if you tend to be ambivalent or have trouble making decisions. If you listen to your heart's desire about daily activities, you will hear its voice in the expressions of your talent.

Appointments with Talent

MATERIALS: Calendar or appointment book (if you don't already have one)

Get a calendar or appointment book that has big open spaces for jotting down each day's activities. Along with your other activities, write in appointments with yourself devoted to talent development. Write the word "talent" in the calendar on each day you wish to make an appointment. Include the specific activity you have chosen for cultivating your talent. This can include reading (this book or other literature pertaining to your talent), working in your Talent Journal, building skills, taking a class, meeting with a mentor, practicing your craft, being in a support group, doing research, etc. Be sure to include the time of day and how long the appointment will last, just as you would in creating any schedule.

Talent Review

A talent review is a way to chart your own progress. This is a time to give and get feedback and answer the question, "How am I doing?" We suggest doing this review at regularly scheduled intervals, such as weekly, biweekly or monthly. Put your talent review schedule in your calendar.

In your talent review, ask yourself the following questions:

- Have I been a good friend to my talent?
- Have I shown up for my appointments with my talent?
- How seriously committed to my talent am I?
- What progress have I made?

If you didn't do so well this week, recommit for next week. Stay with it. If your Inner Critic starts putting you down, just tell it to leave you alone. The same goes for your perfectionist. Remember, slow and steady wins the race.

If you have been faithful to your talent and seen progress, give yourself a treat or celebrate your victories in some way.

Feedback

Do a feedback session in your Talent Journal. Ask yourself the following questions:

- What am I learning about my talent?
- What have I been doing for my talent?
- What do I want to do for my talent?
- What have I learned about myself?
- What have I learned about the way I behave?
- What action do I want to take at this time?

CHAPTER THREE

DEVELOPING TALENT

Raw talent lies dormant, waiting like an unopened birthday present. It's ours, but if we're not using it, there is no benefit to us or anyone else. With nourishment and careful tending, our talent comes to life. As we cultivate this precious gift, talent unwraps itself, revealing more and more abilities. Talent is really an inexhaustible supply of potential, but it needs a partner to develop it. That is your task. Development is the third step in putting your talent to work.

We used to think that classes, mentors, resources and practice were what it took to turn ability into success. Certainly these are essential. However, after many years of experience in career and talent coaching, we have concluded that it takes a great deal more. Technical training and skill-building are not enough. Before these steps can be successful, a foundation of personal qualities must be cultivated.

We have found five key requirements for bringing talent to life. They are:

- courage
- growth
- respect
- persistence
- gratitude

How can we develop these qualities in ourselves? There are no "Courage 101" courses in high schools or colleges. Personal growth seminars rarely focus on talent development. As for respect and persistence, teachers tell students they should have it, but what if they don't? Training in "gratitude" is non-existent, except perhaps in church sermons. Yet if we are serious about putting our talent to work, these five qualities are essential. In this chapter, we provide the tools for nurturing courage, growth, respect for self and for talent, persistence, and an attitude of gratitude.

COURAGE

Bob Hope once said that talent was about Number 10 on the list of what it takes to be successful. Courage was at the top of his list (ours, too). Talent can be sharpened with training and practice, but it takes courage to get the ball rolling. Once we muster up the courage and **act** on our talent, the momentum gathers, carrying us naturally into growth, respect, persistence and gratitude. This is how we mature our talent and put it to work successfully.

Talent without courage is passive: nothing but a dream. Talent fueled by courage turns into **action**. The Latin root for courage is heart. Talent without heart is like a car without gas. With heart, talent becomes spirited and capable of movement. It naturally wants to be expressed.

Ten years ago, Charles was a talented manager in a very successful high-tech company. Although he was respected by executives and exceptionally well paid, Charles was not cut out of the company mold. He observed other managers trying to treat employees like robots, expecting them to dress and think alike. To Charles, this approach seemed counter-productive; he took a different tack. He facilitated growth and treated his staff members as individuals, allowing them to make their own unique and meaningful contributions. As a result, his department stood out as having the highest productivity with the lowest absentee rate in the company. Charles tried to convince the executives that the firm ought to move toward an employee-empowering management style. He demonstrated how it would significantly increase productivity and profits. After many unsuccessful attempts to sway the firm's executives, he decided to consider other options.

Charles set about planning a business of his own as a freelance consultant. His specialty would be building work teams within manufacturing and production companies. He continued working for his employer until he had saved some money and had a few business contacts in place. When he was ready, Charles mustered up all his courage and took the leap. He left his high-paying, secure job to put his dream to the test. Combining talent, experience and vision, he went into business for himself.

Today, Charles's highly successful firm consults for many major corporations, including the very company from which he resigned as manager. Although they saw no need for change 10 years ago, his former employers have since realized the soundness of Charles's approach.

It takes courage to develop talent. We have to truly believe in our talents and be willing to express them. **Courage enables us to act,** to take risks even when we're scared. Courage helps us be responsible for our talent. Courage makes it possible for us to commit to our talent.

Follow Your Heart (Part 1)

MATERIALS: Talent Journal and felt pens

1. With your non-dominant hand, draw a picture of a time when you followed your heart and took a risk that led to more opportunities and growth.

2. With your dominant hand, write about the experience.

   - What were the risks in following my heart?
   - What obstacles did I face (internally and externally)?
   - What did I have to give up?
   - What did I hope to gain?
   - What action did I take?

- How did I feel?
- What were the results?
- In looking back, how do I feel about it?

A time when I followed my heart.

I was engaged to be married. As my wedding date drew near, I became increasingly depressed. I called off the wedding, packed my car with whatever would fit, and moved to California.

I was scared and empowered all at once. I had everything to gain and everything to lose. I was beginning a new life and in the process, I evolved into a different person. Gone was the woman who had tolerated an abusive relationship. Gone was the woman who nurtured herself last.

I stayed with relatives and landed a job within my first month's stay. I struggled emotionally and financially for the first few years—but I survived. I followed the light at the end of the tunnel & made it to the other side—a much happier and more peaceful person.

Follow Your Heart (Part 2)

MATERIALS: Talent Journal or large sheet of paper and felt pens

1. Using your non-dominant hand, draw a big heart. Inside the heart, draw a picture of the talent that you want to develop now. (Optional: You may want to do this as a large picture to be displayed. If so, use a large sheet of art paper.)

2. Consider the talent that you want to develop at this particular time in your life. With your dominant hand, ask the following questions; using your non-dominant hand, write the answers:

   • Is my heart in it?
   • Am I devoted to developing my talent?
   • What could I lose by developing this talent?
   • What might I gain?
   • What action am I willing to take to nurture this talent? (Be very specific here.)
   • How do I feel about embarking on such action?
   • What results do I hope to create?
   • What am I afraid of?
   • Who can help me build up my courage?

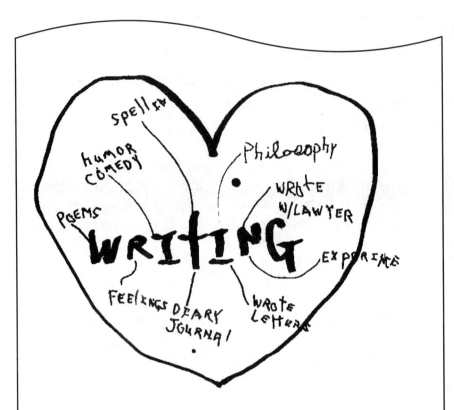

Follow your heart.

Is it in my heart to write?

Yes. Yes. I like sitting down and writing the pages. I love reading what I write and saying that it is good. When the sentences flow, there is a certain good feeling I get.

Devoted to developing the talent?

Not devoted yet. Searching still for the

avenue to pursue. Books, poems, cards. I am looking for a direction now.

What would I lose?

Nothing. No downside. No lifestyle change.

What might I gain?

A feeling of accomplishment, the discipline, feeling intelligent. Knowing only I can write my book. Life is boring unless you do something no one else can do. I am inspired by these words: The worst thing written is better than the greatest thing not written.

Action to take?

I am willing to discipline myself to write. I will set a time to write regularly.

How do I feel?

Excitement. It is very exciting even when I just think about it. It is a risk I want to take. I like risk.

What results do I want to create?

I want to write true-to-life humorous things that other people have also experienced. I want people to say, "Wow, that's just what I thought."

What am I afraid of?

Nothing. No fear, no pressure. I write what I want to. I don't have to do this. I want to write.

GROWTH

Personal growth is fundamental to the development of talent. If you grow your talent, you will automatically be growing yourself. Growth is simultaneously exciting, scary and rewarding. It can also be painful; it moves us out of our comfort zone into the unknown and unfamiliar. We can both attest to the fact that growth often has its painful moments. We have learned to embrace these moments, even though we can't say we like them.

Peggy was an artist in an entertainment-based company and became increasingly interested in the business side of the operation. Electing to move from production artist to estimator, Peggy definitely leaped into foreign territory. As she tells it:

> Working as an estimator required a whole new set of left-brain skills such as analyzing previous costs, researching current processes and forecasting costs on future productions. I knew that estimators spoke English but had no idea what their alphabetical shorthand meant. This was very confusing to me. I felt as if I was traveling in a foreign country.

It was clear that I needed help, so I went desperately looking for a mentor. Fortunately, I found one. She suggested that I picture in my mind every phase of the production process for which I was doing a cost estimate. I knew then exactly what to do. Visualizing each step, I identified time, labor, equipment, supplies, place and exceptions that might occur. With new-found confidence, I continued the leap into unknown territory that had previously intimidated me. My very gracious mentor had taught me an important lesson: start with what you know and then move into the unknown.

Lucia had a similar experience years ago. She left a prestigious design staff position and followed her heart into a job teaching fourth grade in the inner city.

While working on educational exhibits, I developed an interest in teaching methods. I shared this with a teacher I knew. Much to my surprise, I received a call from the elementary school where my friend worked. It was the principal, offering me a job teaching fourth grade. Although I had never taught before, something deep inside told me to take the job. I figured this would be a great hands-on experience. When I expressed doubts due to inexperience, she offered to coach me and provide every possible support. I accepted.

After a couple of weeks in the classroom with 48 children, I began doubting my decision to be a school teacher. It was very hard work managing a classroom full of energetic nine- and ten-year-olds. I was turning into a strict disciplinarian (like the school teachers I had as a kid) and wondering how I had gotten myself into such a mess. I wasn't enjoying it and I wondered how the children could be learning anything.

One day, desperate and ready to quit, I reasoned with myself: *Okay, clearly I don't know anything about teaching; but what DO I know about?* The answer was art and design. The next day, I took all my art supplies to class and set up a table along the side of the room. Any child who finished an assignment early could go paint and draw at the art table. In addition, I began teaching all the curriculum subjects through art. We made photo collages of geography and history using *National Geographic* magazines. The children made their own math materials for learning multiplication and division by drawing and cutting shapes out of colored construction paper. Many of these projects included small teams, so cooperation began to develop.

Soon, discipline problems decreased and everyone's grades improved dramatically. By the end of the semester, the children had won all four prizes in an all-city arts competition sponsored by the board of education. By allowing my old friend the artist-self to partner with the new role of teacher, I turned a chaotic situation into a golden opportunity. My previously gained competence as an artist served as a "hook" for understanding the unfamiliar.

Looking for common threads that unite the known and unknown is conducive to thinking, learning, and participating in a creative and productive way. This is a non-threatening approach to growth. In both cases just described, the learning involved struggle. The stretch into the unknown was often very painful. However, the personal growth and career development that resulted were well worth it.

Just the thought of jumping into the unknown can stop us from developing ourselves. We hear our Inner Critic telling us: *You'll look foolish. You're incapable of succeeding. This is a waste of time.* It is easier to stay in our area of competence and remain comfortable, rather than greet the unknown and embrace life as it happens. The tools you were given in Chapter Two will help you in dealing with that voice inside that puts the brakes on and blocks you from growing.

What most of us fail to remember is this: **the unknown rewards us only when we leap into it**. It takes courage to go into strange new territory. It feels awkward to learn a new skill, like a baby falling down while learning to walk. We need humility to become beginners again. We cannot learn something we already know. By definition, learning consists of the unknown becoming known. The effort transforms into achievement. The talent is put to work.

Visits to the Unknown

MATERIALS: Talent Journal and felt pens

1. Think about the most daring venture into the unknown you ever embarked upon. Pick something you willingly chose to do. Did you accept a new job? Move to a new city? Enter a new relationship? Embark on a course of study? Become a parent? Buy a house? Start a business? Using your non-dominant hand, draw the situation and include yourself in the picture.

2. With your non-dominant hand, write about the situation in your drawing.

   • What prompted you to risk moving into unknown territory in the first place?
   • What feelings did you have upon taking the leap and entering the unknown?
   • What or who helped you in dealing with the unknown?
   • What did you learn about yourself?
   • What talents, skills or insights did you develop as a result of entering the unknown?

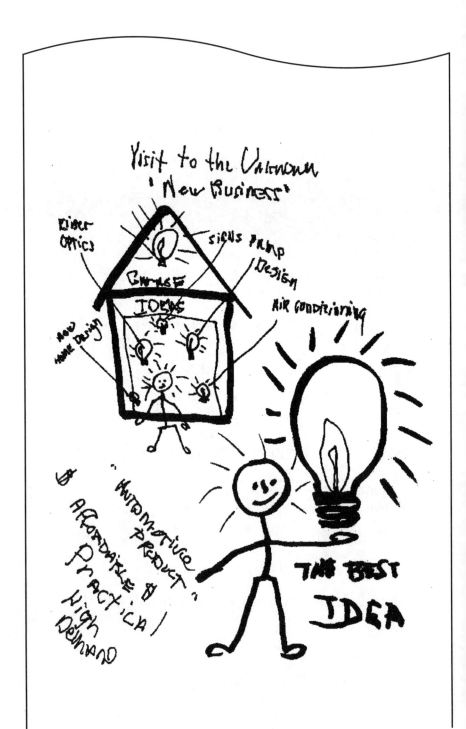

I woke up in the middle of the night thinking about my car. It was brand new—my dream car. How could I make it last a long time? The idea came. It was one of many ideas that I had developed in my garage. It was right then. A voice in my head said: Do it. No one else has done it. Now is the time. Act on it.

I felt a rush. An adrenaline rush. I got excited. I got others excited. Great positive feelings. I created self-momentum. Enormous impact.

My family & my partners helped me. I trust them. They encourage me. Keep my head in the sky with feet on the ground. We talk. They help with course corrections. All aspects are considered. Check this out, check that out. They are my positive healthy advocates.

What I learned was that I found understanding. I am not very reflective but I am more mindful now. I look for the surprises and disappointments. I ask: How am I going to react? I listen, cooperate, collaborate. I am learning my skills. What I am good at. Ideas and production more than resources and business. I don't try to do it all now. Others can help me. I can let them.

I have been to the unknown many times. It is not new to me. I want to be king for a day, a year, forever and make things better. I see what is missing, what is needed, what can be improved. I am not content with mediocre status quo. I want to fix what needs fixing and have the wisdom to know what can't be fixed. I have IDEA talent. The engineer in me knows how to test things. The entrepreneur in me thinks big future ideas. The manufacturer in me builds for efficiency. I have talent for organizing process. I'm an architect at heart. I want to build for the future and save our resources. Everyday ideas lead me to the unknown. It doesn't matter if I am working as an automotive mechanic, building computers, working in construction, real estate or electronic packaging. I have ideas.

We lost our house in the Northridge, California, earthquake on January 17, 1994. I'll never forget that moment— 4:32 A.M.—when the house started shaking. I have never been so terrified in all my life. The house had to be torn down to the ground. With four young children (including a six-month-old baby), to say it was a disaster is putting it mildly. What do we do? Build a new home or let the property go into default and walk away?

We decided to build. Due to a limited budget, I realized I would have to be the designer/contractor. Although I don't have a degree in architecture, I have always been good at building and fixing things. We figured that my experiences working for a building systems company, as well as an architectural firm drafting and constructing scale models, was background enough.

In addition, I had gained supervisory and scheduling skills while working as an office manager for auto repair shops (great preparation for the job of contracting). My responsibilities included buying parts, finding special tools, scheduling specialized mechanics, bookkeeping, etc. A later position as a purchasing agent for my father's firm had further qualified me to contract the building of the house myself. The buying and contracting skills I learned in the corporate environment enabled me to buy the materials for my house at a great discount.

I won't say I wasn't scared. First we had to go through all the red tape of getting the building condemned and torn down. That was a project in itself. I should get a Ph.D. in "bureaucracy" for that job. That left us with only 10 months to build a 3,200-square-foot house. That was when our government rental assistance would run out. I designed the house but hired an architect who could help us with the plans. A contractor friend of mine became my mentor and cheerleader. My husband and his relatives provided the necessary labor force and did most of the actual building. It sure was the hard way to get a new home. On the flip side, the results are well worth it. We built a beautiful new home and we all developed talents, skills and strengths as a result.

In looking back, I see that all the pieces were

In looking back, I see that all the pieces were there. I reassembled my package of talents and skills, and gathered up my support system. This helped me build up the courage and confidence to take on such a monumental project. What I've learned is that I can now do this type of work professionally if I want to. What is more important, I found out that I can accomplish anything I set my heart on.

When we list our visits to the unknown, most of us discover that we are always accompanied by a willingness to learn, stretch and grow. Even when it is *involuntary* and life throws us into the unknown, the result can still be growth. Aleta did not *choose* the Northridge earthquake of 1994. It just happened. However, ultimately she did choose how she was going to respond to the housing dilemma that the quake created. She didn't *have* to design and contract their home. She *chose* to do it, even though she had never built a house before.

Most people who hear Aleta's story gasp in amazement, saying "Wow! What guts. I couldn't possibly do such a thing." That is probably true. The difference is that Aleta knew about her innate talent for architectural design and she was well aware of her other skills that qualified her for the job. She knew it would be a huge stretch, especially given the fast-track schedule, but she was used to being a self-starter and do-it-yourselfer. Hers is a classic example of the adage, "Necessity is the mother of invention." **Courage** is the key. Without it, crisis can paralyze us. With it, we take action.

RESPECT

Remember the popular Aretha Franklin song asking for a little respect? Our unrealized talent sings that song quietly inside our hearts, and it will go on singing it until we listen. The wonderful thing about respecting our talent is that when we do, we respect ourselves as well. A good example is Eleanor McCulley, a vibrant woman who loves her work.

> Eleanor is a nurse with an enormous gift for working with patients who have catastrophic illnesses. She nurtured her talent by listening to its needs, letting it guide her career decisions. Eleanor took every opportunity to develop her talent; studying, teaching and taking assignments no one else wanted.

> When a reduction in nursing staff was about to occur due to declining hospital finances, she repackaged her skills as a health professional. She consulted for organizations seeking wellness programs. Today she consults for a variety of companies on issues that go beyond wellness, including project management and organizational development. By allowing her talent to drive her career path, Eleanor discovered many gifts. She has been a nurse, scientist, researcher, manager, systems analyst and organizational developer. With one book published and more on the way, Eleanor credits her success to respecting her many talents.

Respect for ourselves and for our talent is followed by growth and development. If we value ourselves enough to listen to our innate talent when it speaks to us, we learn to trust that talent to take us where we need to go. Call it destiny, call it whatever you wish. If we respect what our talent is telling us, if we trust it and nurture it, growth is inevitable. Trust, self-nurturing and respect are the nutrients that feed talent.

R-E-S-P-E-C-T (Part 1)

MATERIALS: Talent Journal and felt pens

Write an interview with the talent that wants to emerge. Ask questions with your dominant hand and let the talent respond with your non-dominant hand. Use pens in two contrasting colors. Here are some suggested questions; you can always add to these:

- Please tell me your name. What talent are you?
- What do you need in order to grow and flourish?
- What skills or qualities do I already have that can help you develop?
- What skills or qualities do I need to cultivate to support you?
- Specifically, how do you want to express in my life?

Dialog With Talent

Please tell me your name. What talent are you?

I am you! I am the art in your heart!

What do you need to grow and flourish?

Time.

What skills or qualities do I already have that can help you develop?

You are driven, persistent, you want the best, you want it all. You have desire. You also understand this is not about a product alone. It is also the process. That is why you do it.

What skills or qualities do I need to cultivate to support you?

Patience.

Specifically, how do you want to express in my life?

I want to be the externalization of what is inside you. You fear you can't go deeper—but you must try. I dunno how you do this. You will have to find out for yourself. Do not give up. Keep doing this daily.

I don't know if you are specific enough. Can you say anything else?

Nature is important. Listen to that also.

R-E-S-P-E-C-T (Part 2)

MATERIALS: Collage materials and art paper

On a sheet of art paper, create a magazine photo collage. In the center of your collage, put a picture that symbolizes the talent itself (perhaps a baby, a rosebud, or some other symbol for new growth). Then with magazine photos, illustrate the things your talent told you it needs to grow. Be sure to follow your talent's lead, based on the dialog in Part 1 of this exercise. Respect means LISTENING to your talent.

This collage will be your "visual affirmation" of the actions to take. It will be your guide for developing qualities and building skills that demonstrate respect for your talent.

Display your "visual affirmation" collage someplace where you can see it on a regular basis. Reinforce this positive picture by contemplating it often and burning the image into your brain.

R-E-S-P-E-C-T (Part 3)

MATERIALS: Talent Journal and felt pens

Trust, self-nurturing and respect are best learned from experience, and from those who exemplify these traits in their own lives. Do you know people who are successfully developing their talents? Ask if you can interview them and find out about how they developed their talent. Write your observations in your Talent Journal. You may also want to read biographies or autobiographies of people you admire who have developed their talent. Jot down memorable quotes or phrases from your readings.

PERSISTENCE

Lucia's painting instructor, John Otterson, used to say: *Art is 5 percent inspiration and 95 percent perspiration.* Talent is developed through persistence and hard work. It's as simple as that. Persistence is a key to successfully reaching any goal.

What brings vision to fruition is the driving force of persistence. In our imagination, the sky's the limit, anything is possible. In the "real world," we have to deal with physical laws and limits. Persistence enables us to leap over hurdles, break through blocks and overcome obstacles that come between us and our vision.

Obstacles are both internal and external. Yes, there is an Inner Critic, but there are also very real *outer* circumstances that obstruct the expression of our talent. **Persistence is the key to success.** It enables us to face whatever comes up as we are on our way to the goal. With persistence on our side, we can turn crisis into opportunity, catastrophes into lessons, and obstacles into skill builders. To illustrate this point in her career seminars, Lucia frequently tells one of her favorite stories that she learned in childhood. It is Aesop's fable, *The Tortoise and the Hare.*

> The hare and tortoise were going to run a race. Sounds preposterous. Everyone knows how fast rabbits are with their long hind legs and their ability to jump from spot to spot. The hare was bragging, showing off, putting the tortoise down for being so slow and lumbering. Meanwhile, the tortoise put one foot in front of the other and kept on keeping on. Slow, yes, but persistent to the finish line, which he reached first. Why?
>
> His opponent had copped an arrogant attitude, wasted time, and given no thought or effort to the race. Persistence won the race for the tortoise (not to mention courage, growth and respect for his abilities even when others laughed).
>
> I've never forgotten that story and have lived by it ever since. Years ago, I had to select a large number of staff members in a hurry. One quality I always looked for in job candidates was **persistence**. Would this person collapse at the sight of a big hurdle or unexpected crisis? Or hang in there with dogged determination, solve the problem and reach the goal?

Peggy learned a great deal about persistence from Leona, a former high school administrator.

> Two things troubled Leona deeply. First, she was concerned about the spiritual lives of young people, but she knew that the school was in no position to address this issue. Furthermore, she knew that the school's unhealthy financial situation would eventually result in a staff layoff and she could be among the casualties.

After a great deal of thought, Leona decided to develop her talent for lifting the spirits of children. She created a plan to become a minister. Every morning for nine years she got up at 4:30 to study. In addition, she took two classes a week in spiritual counseling while continuing her full-time position as school administrator. It took diligence, persistence and energy to do this. Leona was asked to work longer hours at school to accommodate cutbacks being made due to financial difficulties. With less time than ever, Leona tenaciously sustained the discipline of her study. She left her position shortly before the school's administrative staff was drastically reduced. She went on to lead her own ministry specializing in children's educational needs.

Persistence means that we simply don't give up. To cultivate this quality, we need to surround ourselves with "finishers," people who demonstrate discipline and determination. These people will keep us inspired. By sharing our concerns during times of low energy or loss of heart, we can keep each other going. Talent will cross the finish line with us in tow if we can prove our staying power.

Mapping the Territory, Staying the Course (Part 1)

MATERIALS: Talent Journal and felt pens

1. Take a large sheet of art paper and place it as a horizontal rectangle.

2. Divide your paper into three sections as shown on the following page. In section 1, using your non-dominant hand, draw a picture of your talent as it is now.

3. In section 3, using your non-dominant hand, draw a picture of your talent after it has blossomed.

4. Now, go back to section 2. Using your non-dominant hand, draw symbols and write phrases representing the blocks you face. Include the obstacles that disrupt you from reaching your talent's full expression as pictured in section 3.

Mapping the Territory, Staying the Course (Part 2)

MATERIALS: Talent Journal and felt pens

In your Talent Journal, write a dialog with the obstacles in your picture. Let the obstacle write with the non-dominant hand, and you write with your dominant hand. Ask the obstacle to tell you about itself. Find out what it wants. Ask it to give you a gift. Then tell the obstacle what you want and what you intend to do about it.

(Note: If there are many obstacles, this may take some time. Start with the obstacle that seems to be causing the most trouble right now. Then do the dialogs with the other obstacles later.)

Dialog with Time

Time, tell me a little bit about yourself. Who are you?

The big T is who I am! The Terrible T! You can't fool me! You'll see! Okay — you never have enough of me — I'm your curse! Look at doing these exercises—you said: I don't have time! Here it is—three days before it is due. Shame on you.

The Truth is—another T word—you don't manage me very well. You go off on your tangents and I get away from you. You cannot do everything. That's greedy.

So, Time, what do you want from me?

To be more practical. Prioritize more. I want you also to try to find some balance. Don't rush things. Some things need me.

Time—I want you to give me a gift. You choose. Will you give me one? What will it be?

All you want is more of me. Greedy. Needy. Okay. Here it is.

One day weekly, get out of the house and play; do something different. Not printmaking. It's Okay. Use this card. Of course, you'll have to do some planning in order to use it.

Well, thanks, Time. It is nice of you to give me your "okay" to play. I will give it my best shot.

Okay so now from you I want . . . I want . . . you to just ease up on me a little. Maybe <u>you</u> need an "okay to play" card. How about a vacation? You (and I too, I'll admit) are full of excuses. People are tired

of hearing them. I need you to help me plan.
Let's do it every Sunday. Okay? Let's
plan our week every Sunday morning.

GRATITUDE

Gratitude nourishes our talent. Gratitude is an attitude of thankfulness. It can best be described as a *state of grace*. Why? Gratitude *opens us up* and enables us to accept ideas and perceptions. This receptivity is essential to the development of our talent. A personal life crisis taught Lucia the value of gratitude, and how finding and developing talent can be an act of thanksgiving.

Illness struck and I had no choice but to surrender to my body's need to rest and heal. Since medical intervention was completely ineffective, I desperately turned inward for guidance. I found it right under my own nose, in my journal. I discovered that simply writing and drawing my feelings and experiences out helped me tremendously. Not only did I feel better physically, I also felt empowered through this incredible form of emotional release. After a while, I healed from the illness that was later diagnosed as a collagen (connective tissue) disease.

After my complete recovery, I realized that the illness had really been a beautiful gift in disguise. It was through my illness that I discovered a whole range of creative techniques for healing body, mind and spirit. My gratitude for this gift of healing led me to a new career. A Higher Power had made me the custodian of these tools for healing. I felt it was my responsibility to share them with others, which is what I have been doing for the past two decades.

The Talent Fairy Godmother (Part 1)

MATERIALS: Collage supplies

1. On a sheet of art paper, create a photo collage and/or drawing. Your subject: the Talent Fairy Godmother.

2. Put the picture up in a special place so that you can remember to give thanks for the blessing of your gifts and talents.

The Talent Fairy Godmother (Part 2)

MATERIALS: Talent Journal and felt pens

1. Write out a conversation with your Talent Fairy Godmother. Use two contrasting colors, one for you and one for the Talent Fairy Godmother. The Talent Fairy Godmother writes with your non-dominant hand; you write with your dominant hand.

2. Using your dominant hand, write a thank-you letter to your Talent Fairy Godmother. Let her know how grateful you are for her assistance and guidance in growing your talent. Ask for her guidance and assistance in any particular area of your talent's development.

Dear Talent Fairy Godmother,

Thank you so much for your guidance in naming, accepting and developing my talent. I need help with overcoming the roadblocks with Time, Inner Critic and Money. Will you help me?

Of course I will! I am here to support you and get you through negative feelings and comments from Critic. Together, we will do your heart's desire. I will help you.

Thank you. I'm sure I'll be back tomorrow asking for something.

Look closely at how you honor your talent. Talent serves you only if it is nourished. Just like physical exercise, growing your talent takes time and practice. Schedule it into your life.

Taking Time for Talent

MATERIALS: Talent Journal and felt pens

1. With your dominant hand, write out an agreement to make journal entries on a regular basis. It doesn't have to be done every day. We've found that a consistent routine is the most effective. For example: every Monday and Thursday at 8:00 P.M. This can include doing the exercises or simply writing your reflections on what you are learning about talent. You may also want to record recent experiences that relate to talent.

   We suggest choosing the same time each day for the sake of establishing journal-keeping as a habit. Journaling (the word comes from French for day) is an excellent way to practice persistence and discipline in the service of your talent. Making time for talent demonstrates your commitment. The Talent Journal is a perfect vehicle for expressing that commitment.

The *amount* of time you devote to your Talent Journal is your choice. Those who devote at least 15 minutes per day usually experience noticeable progress. After a while, journaling will grow into a good habit. Once you get going and see the results, you may want to spend even more time with your Talent Journal.

2. In your Talent Journal, re-state the particular talent(s) that you are developing at this time. Be specific. Then write out what you are doing to develop your talent by way of training, practice, skill-building, mentoring, etc. Give yourself a reward for being willing to serve your talent.

Contract

I agree to work in my Talent Journal twice a week for half an hour, on Mondays & Thursdays at 3 P.M. I agree to do this until I have completely recuperated from the accident and found a new career direction.

The talents I want to develop are in financial investing. I am taking a correspondence course in investments. It requires me to research, calculate figures, track information, conceptualize & analyze.

I am reading all the currently published bestselling books on investing and the market as well as the recommended classics. I am learning about the market's history. I am studying successful investing companies and reading about individuals who have been successful in investments.

As I am able, I plan to take a class at the local college and will interview people who work as stockbrokers. My reward is the excitement I feel about going into a different field from real estate development and project management. One that is less physically taxing and that is mentally stimulating for me.

Reading is easy. Talk is cheap. **Action** is the key to success. World-renowned designer/inventor R. Buckminster Fuller used to say: "The action you take within 24 hours after getting an idea or vision spells the difference between success or failure." Are you ready to act, to do "a little something" every day for your talent? Keep it simple. Remember the tortoise. Slow and steady wins the race. Put your talent on your calendar. Schedule it in like everything else that is important to you. Make talent a priority, and it will reward you in return.

TALENT WORKOUT

Heart's Desire
Have you been developing the habit of asking about your **heart's desire** regarding your everyday life?

Talent Review
Have you been making and keeping **regular appointments** devoted to your talent? Have you been keeping your Talent Journal on any regular basis (weekly, daily)?

Feedback
Do a feedback session in your Talent Journal. Ask yourself the following questions:

- What am I learning about my talent?
- What have I been doing for my talent?
- What do I want to do for my talent?
- What have I learned about myself?
- What have I learned about the way I behave?
- What action do I want to take at this time?

CHAPTER FOUR

MATCHING TALENT TO NEEDS

When talent fills a need, it begins to define our behavior. The challenge is to identify needs. Someone once said: Define the problem, and the solution will follow. We say, "Define the need, and the talent to fill it will follow." But the question still remains: Where and how do we find needs? Like talent, needs are right under our noses in everyday life. When looking for needs, pay close attention to complaints, wishes and necessity. These are the places where you are most likely to find needs.

COMPLAINTS

Everyone is good at complaining. We do it all the time. We know what we *don't* want, but all too often we can't say what we *do* want. In looking for needs, listen to what people complain about. A good place to start is with yourself. What things do you complain about the most? Is it services, products or systems? What is it that doesn't work for you? What action would you take if it would make a difference?

> Marla, the mother of three young children, was very dissatisfied with the educational system in her community. Her children attended the local public school and they all complained about how boring their classes were. Marla was concerned and met with the teachers. She was told: "There are too many special needs students and we don't have adequate resources to handle them. Some of the kids should be in accelerated classes, but we're understaffed and we can't accommodate them. We just have to make the best of it."

> Other parents were as concerned as Marla. Together they became active in a PTA volunteer program, providing more parent assistance in the classroom. It soon became clear that this approach helped somewhat but didn't really solve the problem. Their children were still complaining about being bored.

Marla was frustrated with the situation and decided to search for a solution. She contacted Raymond and Lakisha, two old friends from college days who had gone on to become language arts educators. They had been developing some innovative teaching methods. When Marla sought their advice, they said they had been looking for a school where they could try out their ideas.

The university where Lakisha and Raymond were teaching got a research grant to pilot their program and Marla's district agreed to host the project. The team was able to test their ideas out in the very classrooms Marla had been complaining about. The classrooms were just as understaffed as before, but the new teaching methods answered the needs of the students. Academic scores increased dramatically in all grades. This research project also had a strong parent involvement component built into it, which added tremendously to the strength of the program.

Another ripe area for finding out about people's unmet needs is in complaints about service. We often hear people complaining about lack of courteous service. We live in a high-tech era in which companies are shifting from personalized service to automated systems. This can have a negative impact on customers as well as employees of the company.

When a company implements or upgrades its phone system, chaos can result. Not only does a new untested system interrupt the company's operation, but it causes confusion for customers. We often hear the complaint: "I can't believe it. I navigated my way around the phone information system for 15 minutes and ended up right where I started." Some of these system problems even have nicknames, such as *phone maze* or *voice mail jail*. Sometimes we experience internal service problems. We know a man who complained about problems with service on the job.

Gary worked for a tool and dye company. His department had to get most of its supplies from the warehouse and tool crib. Gary consistently had a hard time getting the supplies he needed. He also found out that his department was getting back-charged exorbitant rates for the supplies he did use. This, in turn, increased his costs quite a bit. Gary searched for better deals from outside vendors and was able to find much lower prices. He also looked into prices that the company was paying for the supplies they had in the warehouse. Again, he found that the costs were quite high. Gary realized that since his company had other departments that were also buying tools and supplies, it would make sense to establish a cooperative buying program to save money. After all, he had secured good deals for his projects; why not get them for the company at large?

Armed with all this information, Gary approached his manager with a new purchasing plan. The response was, "We've always done it this way and we're going to continue doing it this way." End of subject. So, without making a big issue out of it, Gary continued placing his own orders with outside vendors. As a result, he was always under budget for supplies on his projects. His peers, noticing this, asked how he did it. To help them, Gary began placing orders for them. When the manager found out, he reprimanded Gary. "You're spending too much time placing orders and not enough time on the bench," the manager told him, and then presented him with a memo. "Stop doing independent ordering! You'll lose your job if you don't."

Gary took the letter to a company executive along with a record of all his savings. He included the original plan for cooperative buying that had been rejected by his manager. The executive was impressed and offered Gary a position in purchasing. In the process of reorganizing its supply services, Gary made an interesting discovery. Not only had the company been paying top dollar for supplies, but some managers were getting kickbacks from vendors that drove costs even higher. Gary has become very successful in purchasing and has developed sophisticated tracking and quality control systems that have been adopted by other divisions of the company. It all started with grumbling about poor service from the warehouse and tool crib.

Complaints about **products** that don't work are just as commonplace as complaints about service. "This car is a lemon. That brand stinks. This is a pile of junk." Bad products inspire jokes and epithets, and create much frustration. TV advertising feeds on the image of the competitive product as flawed, inadequate, too expensive, etc. Advertisers manufacture complaints about competitive products, hoping to discourage customers from buying them. In a mad scramble for your dollar, advertisers come right out and name the competitor, along with specific data on how inferior its product is. We're all familiar with car commercials and ads for long-distance phone services that tarnish the competition with "facts" and figures. This was unheard of in the past, when comparisons with "Brand X" were about as specific as advertisers ever got about their competitors.

Bad products and inadequate services catalyze our talents. When people are dissatisfied, it is usually because a need is not being met. The idea is to match talents to needs. Sometimes the need can even be our own. On a trip to Indonesia, Peggy had the pleasure of meeting Rachel, a successful woman who had developed an entire business because of dissatisfaction with a particular type of product. Here is Rachel's story:

> My two sisters and I had stable 9-to-5 jobs as support personnel with prospering companies. The truth is, we were all dying of boredom. After work we'd often meet to have dinner together. The two topics of conversation were usually how bored we were at work, and how difficult it was to find clothes we really liked. We all prefer flowing, feminine styles that can be dressed up or down with accessories. We enjoy creating our own "look." At the time, most stores were showing tailored fitted suits and dresses with micro-miniskirts.
>
> While vacationing together in Indonesia, we discovered we could have any style reproduced inexpensively by local dressmakers in just a few days. That really intrigued us and we set about buying fabric, drawing up variations on our favorite outfits and patiently waiting for the results. Without

exception, each creation turned out perfectly. We had found a shopping oasis.

On the trip home, we talked nonstop about setting up our own business. We would offer a service to small dress shops by researching the clientele's preferences and creating a product line for the store. We wanted to specialize in getting hard-to-find items. It took us less than six months to formulate our business plan, do the market research, borrow the start-up capital and go off to Indonesia again.

Today the sisters have a booming import business. Along with clothing, their line also includes fashion accessories, gift items and artwork. They have little time to be bored and less time for complaining. They obviously had a talent for shopping, which has now become "buying for the business." Most important, they all love what they do *and* what they wear.

Discovering Needs:
Complaint Department

MATERIALS: Talent Journal and felt pens

1. In your Talent Journal, create two columns. Label the first column "Complaint" and the second column "Need."

Complaint   **Need**

In column 1, with your dominant hand, make a list of all the things you gripe about (to yourself or others). These are the constant complaints about anything in your life: long lines at the bank, your car that's always breaking down, your neighbor's stereo blasting away in the wee hours, your kid's messy room, the cost of living, your job, your marriage, etc.

2. In column 2, with your non-dominant hand, write out the need that each complaint is pointing to. Example: Noisy neighbors at night—I need to sleep and can't.

3. Read your list over. Then on a new page, with your dominant hand, draw a picture of your primary complaint.

4. On the next page, draw the solution to that complaint, using your non-dominant hand. Show yourself with your needs being met.

Complaint	Need
My work	More money & become a manager
My appearance	Physically fit and less fat
Traffic jams when I am working	To deliver certain jobs without stress
Work relationship	To have the work done correctly and in a timely way
Physical pain	To be healthy and free of pain

COMPLAINTS OF OTHERS

Another excellent place to find unfulfilled needs is in the complaints of *others*. Most of us prefer to do the complaining rather than listen to others complain. However, the dissatisfactions of others can be a rich source of needs that our talent can fill. Madison Avenue knows this. Billions of dollars are spent each year to *create* a need that might not already exist. Why? So that, whether you really *need* it or not, you will *want* the advertiser's product enough to buy it. As mentioned above, advertising often sets you up to complain about the product you're already using. If you're dissatisfied, you're likely to switch brands.

Needs are often camouflaged in complaints. We know two entrepreneurs who built a business because they listened to complaints.

Matt and Warren had both worked as salesmen, but for different companies. They had been searching for a business they might create together, although they weren't sure exactly what it was. They spent a lot of time entertaining all kinds of ideas and possibilities. Their friends and families had heard these discussions for so long, they thought nothing would ever come of it.

After their companies both moved to the same building in a new downtown office complex, the two friends began to hear complaints about the janitorial service. Floors were grimy and restrooms weren't properly maintained. A year passed and the complaints worsened. One day over lunch, Warren and Matt discussed the situation and wondered, "How difficult can it be to provide competent janitorial service for this complex?" They realized a business opportunity was staring them right in the face. This was a perfect opportunity for the friends to work together.

The two men bought some janitorial equipment and convinced the owner of the building to try them out for one month. As moonlighters, they hired several unemployed kids they knew and put them to work, closely supervising the quality of the service. For the first time, there were no complaints from the tenants. The two partners arranged a short-term contract, training more unemployed kids and some family members.

Word spread to managers of other buildings in the complex that there was a good, reliable janitorial service available. Warren and Matt agreed to take on a few more clients. However, they elected to draw the line there, stay small and maintain the highest quality service. It paid off. Both are now retired from their sales jobs and work full time managing their janitorial service.

Identifying Needs:
From Demand to Supply (Part 1)

MATERIALS: Talent Journal and felt pens

With your dominant hand, write about a time when you identified a need that someone had and you helped fill it. What was the need? Was the other person aware of this need? If so, how did the person express it? If the person wasn't aware of it, did you point it out? What did you do to help fill the person's need?

I work with landscape and there is a current demand (and real need) for water conservation. I have worked for large companies that have paid huge amounts in penalties. They see the need and basically think conservation of water is "a nice thing to do." But it wasn't until they got hit with large penalties, some as high as 250 thousand dollars, that they really started to pay attention to it.

One company had developed property with 325 homes, and its 20-year old landscape began to visually deteriorate. There were ocean views to be considered and a number of trees to be considered as well. Some people wanted to cut the trees down to create more ocean views. I was faced with having to explain the need for selective cutting and translating the need so that everyone bought into it. Selective cutting would create the views that people wanted and thin out the trees (which would help restore the landscape to a healthy balanced system).

Doing the tree work is easy. It's convincing people with different values that's hard. In this case, people were confusing their wants with needs. I had to persuade them and sell them on this idea of selective cutting.

Identifying Needs: From Demand to Supply (Part 2)

MATERIALS: Talent Journal and felt pens

1. Think about a situation in your life today in which someone you know has a need. How would you identify this need? With your non-dominant hand, write it down.

2. Can you think of any way in which you could help the person meet this need? Do you have any talents, abilities, skills or information that could be applied in this situation? Can you refer the person with the need to someone who can fill it? With your non-dominant hand, write it down.

Currently I'm working to identify a treatment for a tree disease. A company just called me to help them figure out what to do. They planted hundreds of one kind of tree and the disease is threatening all the trees. They could lose their entire landscape.

The disease had affected other plants. I had to do a history on the disease. It was first recorded in the late 1800s and has surfaced in 30-year cycles. I always begin by doing a history; it tells me a great deal about the situation or need. My approach is to find a way to treat the problem, so I need lots of information.

The best way for me to help in this situation was to find a treatment. The others who had been brought in to help wanted to destroy the trees. They have a different mind-set.

mind-set. You have to prove that treatment is possible. This means doing research, reports, task calendars, process layouts in programs. You have to establish a rhythm of activity and new habits.

The skills I bring are physically knowing how to do the work, pitching in and doing the work, training others, being multilingual, having rapport skills and having a deep understanding of landscape, which comes from my expertise in turf, soil, trees, shrubs and flowers. I have an ability to see the whole picture, to see things in their proper context and to understand how they interrelate, link together and affect each other. I am an environmentalist. I went to school to learn how to put it all together. My industry separates its disciplines; I bring them together. I don't generally recommend others because I like filling the

> *needs myself. I can do the diagnostic work required and find the treatment/solution.*

WISHES

When we are not complaining, we are often **wishing.** "I wish my job weren't so boring. I wish there wasn't so much violence in this city. I wish I had more money. I wish I didn't have so many debts. I wish my back didn't hurt all the time. I wish I could lose 20 pounds." On and on it goes. Needs are often masquerading as wishes. This is not only true of our wishes, but the wishes of others as well.

Many of us dismiss wishes. "That's just a pipe dream, a flight of fantasy. It's impossible—it'll never happen." We learned from others that wishes and daydreams were a waste of time. Our parents said things like: "Get practical! That's really childish. What a daydreamer." We criticize people who spend time wishing for this or that. "Dreams are for kids," we say. "Let's get *real* here." Of course, living mostly in a world of wishes that never come true is not advisable and can indicate pathology. However, by dismissing our wishes, we lose something very important. We fail to observe the seeds of needs lying buried in our desires. Wishing can point to **needs** wanting to be recognized.

The dictionary tells us that wish, desire, want and need are all interchangeable, depending upon the usage. Your wishes and desires may unfold for you a new and entirely possible reality. Ralph Waldo Emerson once said: "Be careful what you set your heart on for it will surely be yours." Wishes lead us to needs that are waiting to be filled by talent. Peggy likes to tell people about her good friend Vonda, an example of someone who turned wishes into reality.

We used to sit on Vonda's living room floor looking through travel brochures, making plans for the day when we could afford such adventures. We preferred exotic and unusual places that were not in the mainstream for most travel agencies. Vonda was very well-read and steeped in the mythology of ancient and lost cultures. She wanted to find a way to bring these cultures alive by taking travelers to ruins that still exist today.

It didn't take Vonda long to make the leap from wishing to actually becoming a travel consultant. She went on a tour and learned everything she could from watching the guides as well as talking with the other travelers.

For her next journey, Vonda volunteered to help the organizer develop the itinerary and assisted the tour guide on the trip. She had a wonderful time. This experience provided her with even more information about creating, organizing and implementing such trips. Upon returning home, she discovered other people, like herself, who were attracted to exotic places and ancient sites. She eventually started her own business. It was a courageous act, but Vonda stepped out and did it. Today, she has her own company, customizing tours for a very satisfied clientele.

Undoubtedly, there will be many more successful trips for Vonda and more lessons in risk-taking, visioning and organizing both people and programs. She is a wonderful example of someone who listened to needs and put her talent to work filling them.

Filling the Needs:
Make a Wish . . . (Part 1)

MATERIALS: Talent Journal and felt pens

1. With your dominant hand, make a wish list. Include all areas of your life: work, hobbies, personal relationships, recreation, health, etc.

2. Prioritize your wish list, from the most significant to the least important, by placing a number in the left-hand margin.

Priority	Wish List
1	• I want to be financially independent, on my own
5	• More free time to read, clean, garden, walk, play with dog, exercise
2	• Work that is extremely satisfying
11	• Travel to spas / retreats at least once per year

7   • A beautiful home in the
       mountains where I work
       and play

8   • A soul-mate relationship
       with one who shares this
       space

3   • Healthy, vigorous energy

10   • Dry, sunny climate, the
       smell of pine needles on
       a warm day

9   • Using aromatherapy,
       herbs, fitness to take
       people to better places
       in their lives

4   • Golden retrievers around
       me at work & play

6   • Beautiful music, serenity

Filling the Needs:
Make a Wish . . . (Part 2)

MATERIALS: Talent Journal and felt pens or collage materials

1. From Part 1 of this activity, select the most important wish and draw a picture of it having come true. Be sure to put yourself in the picture.

   Note: You may want to do this as a large collage on art paper.

2. With your non-dominant hand, write about your "wish picture." Write out your description in the present tense as if your wish had already become a physical reality.

   • Where are you?
   • Whom are you with?
   • What are you doing?
   • How do you feel now that your dream has come true?
   • What strengths have you developed in the process?

pt 1e Me-My Wish-Living It

Me — My Wish — Living It

I am working independently, attracting
abundance into my life. I feel confident,
balanced. I am able to take steps to change
whenever I feel it necessary. I'm no longer
hampered financially . . . a sense of ease
comes over me. Things are never a struggle,

just obstacles that become challenges and fun. I feel <u>in control</u> of my life; it's <u>glorious</u>. I attract special people and circumstances as I radiate this feeling.

I am working at home with dog and loved ones. The setting is gorgeous, in a mountain community. I have time for all my loves — working, gardening, walking, enjoying the outdoors and my house. I work on new ways of helping enrich others' lives and have tremendous satisfaction from it. I find myself writing about these things.

I find I have arrived at this quiet, flowing place. Having felt the spiritual connection to actually living my thoughts in action is quite beautiful. I find myself in "grace." A feeling of being blessed and showered with radiant light. It is as if the heavens have opened up. The exhilaration and energy are magnificent.

Other people's wishes are an excellent place to look for needs. Listen carefully to what people wish for. Pay attention and you may find a vehicle for sharing your talent by helping someone's wishes come true.

It was right after the big Southern California earthquake of 1994. Mark, an experienced building contractor, kept hearing the same thing wherever he went. "I wish I knew more about home construction and repair," or "I wish I knew someone I could *trust* who could give me some solid advice about the damage to my home and about repairing it." Mark knew there were plenty of ambulance-chasing, unethical or incompetent contractors and other people in the building trades taking advantage of quake victims. Mark even encountered some of these opportunists, who were saying things like, "Wow! Is there *money* to be made out there. We're gonna get rich off this quake." Mark knew that homeowners had a right to be concerned. They were fair game for any unscrupulous contractors.

This gave Mark an idea. Wouldn't it be great to create an information network helping earthquake victims assess the damage to their homes? When Mark shared his idea with his subcontractors, they all went for it. They started spreading the service by word of mouth, volunteering to go look at damaged property and educate homeowners. They offered to review any estimates from contractors, checking to see if they were legitimate and if their prices were fair. Mark and his group offered their services free of charge and did not take any jobs they consulted on, to avoid conflict of interest. They wanted to help people in need.

Before long, this contractor and his associates got calls for more paying jobs than they could handle. However, they managed to fit the free consultations into their very busy schedules. This led to referrals to homeowners who did not have earthquake damage but simply wanted remodels or additions by competent, honest workers. The referrals came from people whom they had helped for free. In the process, Mark discovered that he enjoyed consulting. He currently offers consulting services as part of his business. However, there is still no charge for earthquake victims.

Helping Others

MATERIALS: Talent Journal and felt pens

Have you ever helped someone's wishes come true? How? With your dominant hand, write about it in your talent journal.

I had a 30-year-old man in adult school who wanted a job with the Fire Dept. He had taken the written exam 4 or 5 times and repeatedly failed the math part of the test. He told me that he did not know his multiplication tables and couldn't do math. He told me he had tried flash cards and taping 3 or 4 combinations to his car visor in an effort to memorize the tables on the way to work. It didn't work for him.

I counseled him by saying that there were other ways of learning. He was trying to learn math by reading and memorizing. This is great for a visual learner, but he wasn't a visual learner.

I suggested he use toothpicks as a kinesthetic aid in learning to multiply. I had him pick a combination like 3 x 5 and count out three separate piles of five toothpicks each. He then put the toothpicks in one pile, counting them as he made the single pile. This kinesthetic approach worked. Practicing these techniques each day, he learned his multiplication tables.

The next challenge was to pass the math test. I got an old copy of the test and we studied from it. With his new-found confidence, the rest was easy. He successfully passed the test and is currently employed as a fireman.

NECESSITY

Sometimes, necessity is the messenger of need. Aleta's story about the earthquake that suddenly and catastrophically created their need for housing is a perfect case in point. Necessity certainly mothered Aleta's talents as a designer/contractor. Necessity usually brings pressing needs to our attention so dramatically that we simply cannot ignore them. Necessity often accompanies misfortune and creates opportunity.

We all face crisis at one time or another in our lives. Looking at how you have identified needs that arose from a past crisis is a valuable way to train yourself to look for current needs. Without realizing it, you have been exercising this skill all along. You simply may not have been consciously aware of it. If you aren't clear about what the needs are, you cannot respond to them. The next journal activity will guide you in pinpointing the needs that your talent can fill.

Necessity Calls, Talent Answers (Part 1)

MATERIALS: Talent Journal and felt pens

Think about a time when you were confronted with a crisis and rose to the occasion, survived, and gained from the experience.

With your dominant hand, write about this crisis, asking yourself:

- How did I feel when the event happened or the situation occurred?
- What went through my mind?
- What needs did the situation reveal or create?

- What did I do to get those needs met?
- What did I learn about myself?
- What talents, abilities or strengths revealed themselves because of this crisis?

I've been involved in designing and installing booths at trade shows and other events. My first international show taught me a lot. I had an idea about the electrical differences between countries and I had tried to plan ahead.

When I got to the show I found that I had to deal with all kinds of differences. The major problem was that nobody's plugs worked. The Italian contractor had one kind of plug system. We were in France, where there is another plug system. The English brought their own (as did everyone else) and I had Edison from the U.S., with a different plug system and a different voltage & cycle system.

When nothing worked, I knew I just had to start constantly adapting and keeping a "reality eye" on what was happening.

There was mass confusion with all the different languages, not to mention the systems. For example, one Italian company had a Japanese owner who spoke more English than Italian. My reaction was to start doing.

When a problem or crisis hits, I let go of the stress and start doing. I ask myself: What needs to be done? What has to happen? What will it take to make it work?

I learned that planning ahead pays off. In my first job I ended up transforming everything to the U.S. system. In later years, I figured out what could be done. I discovered that the French end could be spliced to an Italian end to get the power going. But planning ahead is the key.

To meet the need, I asked myself: What resources do I have? What is available locally? Who can I find with experience in doing this?

What I learned was that sometimes, when you look around to find a guy to help, the only place you find him is in the mirror. I learned the guy in the mirror is my best resource.

I am creative in that I can design, conceptualize, develop design, prototype design & sketch. My technical background includes craftsmanship, electrical and mechanical fabrication, engineering, hydraulics, pneumatics, drafting, machine shop practices (welding, lathes, mills) and knowledge of materials. My multi-talented background surfaced in that situation.

Necessity Calls,
Talent Answers (Part 2)

MATERIALS: Talent Journal and felt pens

1. Are you confronting a situation at this time in your life that calls for some creative problem-solving? With your dominant hand, draw a picture of the situation. Be sure to include yourself in the picture.

2. With your non-dominant hand, draw a picture of yourself *after* successfully dealing with the situation, solving the problem, resolving the issue.

3. Look at your second picture. With your dominant hand, write about it in your journal in the present tense. Imagine that you've solved the problem already and are answering the following questions:

   • How do I feel about myself?
   • What talent have I developed in the process of solving the problem?
   • What skills do I have that can be applied in new situations that arise?

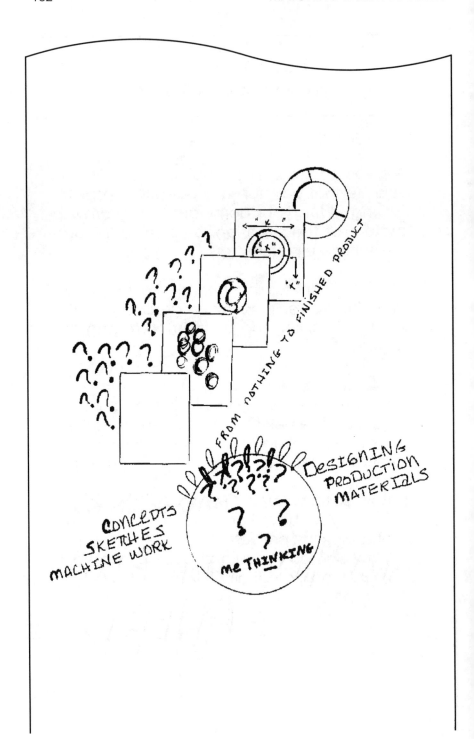

I am currently designing prototype film parts for a filmmaker who has identified some needs. He wanted someone who could work creatively with his needs and specifications. I feel great satisfaction getting it done. Starting with nothing and getting to the end result that everyone wanted is the end of the job—happiness. I like to get it done quick & get to the next job. It could be better & more fun than the last.

I'm using my design background in engineering, as well as my practicality and skill with materials (plastics & metals). All these skills relate to each other. They all need sharpening with each challenge. I am always learning about materials—that never stops. These skills can be applied to all the work that I do.

ACTION

This week, find two or three people you know who have their own business or who are selling a product or service. Ask these people the following questions:

- What need are you filling with your product or service?
- How did you know about this need in the first place?
- How did you get started meeting this need?
- What challenges did you face?
- What do you enjoy most about your work?
- What talents do you have that make it possible for you to do your work?
- What skills have you had to develop?

TALENT WORKOUT

Heart's Desire
Have you been developing the habit of asking about your **heart's desire** regarding your everyday life?

Talent Review
Have you been making and keeping **regular appointments** devoted to your talent? Have you been keeping your Talent Journal on any regular basis (weekly, daily)?

Feedback
Do a feedback session in your Talent Journal. Ask yourself the following questions:

- What am I learning about my talent?
- What have I been doing for my talent?
- What do I want to do for my talent?

• What have I learned about myself?
• What have I learned about the way I behave?
• What action do I want to take at this time?

Day Before Valentine's

This sunny day I gave myself and my developing talent a gift—I broke out a beautiful journal I have saved for years. In it I described my journey to use my talents as fully as possible. I quoted Ch. 3 on Persistence and Gratitude. I wrote a play-by-play of recent efforts to utilize my talent in a speculative career effort, and how pleased and surprised I was by my speedy success! I will continue to chart and record my efforts and the positives I pile up with persistent efforts—small and large. I'll use it to refresh me when I'm discouraged, to jump-start me & fuel my drive and forward motion as I work to develop my talents.

CHAPTER FIVE

PUTTING TALENT TO WORK

The downsizing of American business and government projects has thrown many people into turmoil about their occupations. Traditional job security and confidence in employers is becoming a thing of the past. Workers are having to develop more flexibility and self-responsibility. The way to go about this is to find out **what you are good at, what you enjoy most and how you can make a living doing it.** It is a strategy for survival as well as fulfillment.

It is clear that self-responsibility is gaining greater acceptance. Just visit the business section of any bookstore. There are countless titles proclaiming that career-seekers need to: "work with passion, do what you love, find meaningful work." A couple of decades ago, finding a job was the issue; finding *meaning* or *joy* in one's work was rarely discussed. Today we see record-breaking increases in start-up business.

Growing Your Career

Talent needs an **opportunity** to express itself and to mature. Talent loves to solve problems, overcome challenges and invent something new. This usually reveals itself first in our personal lives: interests, hobbies, avocations and daily life situations (cooking, auto repair, decorating, dressing, managing money). Then it transfers over into work and career. Of course, retirement occupations are also a vehicle for talent. These may be voluntary instead of paid jobs, but have the same qualities as a career (growth, skill development, contribution to society and a sense of achievement and fulfillment).

Making a living provides the greatest opportunity for talent to bloom. Talent loves to go to work. Career is the perfect arena for developing and expressing our innate abilities. After all, we spend a large percentage of our lives on the job. Whether we are employed by someone else or working for ourselves, our talent should have room to play in the workplace.

How talent shapes our careers depends upon our beliefs and expectations about work. These are learned from our family, peers, role models, teachers and the media. While we are influenced by the generations that came before us, it is important to realize that they grew up in a very different world than we did. Each of us must redefine for ourselves what it means to make a living. The question is, what does "career" mean to you?

We all participate in creating our own career paths. This occurs in two ways. Either our job happens to us and we passively go along for the ride, or we listen to our heart's desire and cultivate our dream. Passively waiting for "the economy" to improve or "the dream job" to find us is no way to live. It breeds a "poor me" victim attitude and robs us of our sense of intrinsic worth and our self-esteem.

You may be asking, "How do I chart my own career direction?" The answer is: **vision**, **intention**, **goal** and **action**. By this we mean having a dream, deciding to go for it, setting specific goals and tasks and following through on them. You may like or dislike any given result, but each action and its result is a stepping stone toward realizing your dream. Each action you take will also develop you as a person.

Creating your unique career path requires that you, as the Canadian aboriginal women put it, "Know who you are, how you behave and what actions you need to take." Knowledge about yourself is of primary importance.

As our external security systems continue to weaken, the internal systems must be developed and fortified. Although easy to discount, these "softer" internal values assist us in forming our abilities and character. When you organize your career around your talents, you will make an inward journey that allows you the fullest possible expression in the outer world.

TALENT AS CAREER COACH

People with talent-based career paths tell us that when they are unable to use their talent, they often experience depression, stress-related illness or anxiety. If they listen to the "symptoms" as messages from their talent, they can usually get back on track.

Laurene began drawing at about age four. As she grew older, she gained a reputation as a "talented artist" wherever she went. It was a natural progression from self-taught amateur to art student to professional artist. Laurene especially loved exploring new ways of doing things technically, and eventually became an expert on art materials and production processes such as printmaking for commercial and fine art application.

A manufacturer of art supplies had so much respect for Laurene's expertise and willingness to push the boundaries of its product, that the company asked her to be its representative. She agreed and traveled extensively, demonstrating as well as troubleshooting the product line. At first, Laurene enjoyed the change of pace and variety of places she visited. However, as time went on, she found herself doing less art and more lecturing and administrative paper-pushing. With each trip she experienced increasing fatigue and even anxiety.

Back home for the Christmas holidays, Laurene sat down one day and took stock of her life. Something pulled her over to her small studio, which had been sorely neglected. She began playing around with materials and exploring new possibilities. After a few hours immersed in the art process, Laurene's anxiety and vague discomfort lifted as if by magic. Laurene suddenly realized that she needed to draw and to produce art to feel good. The anxiety had been nothing more than a signal that something was wrong. Time for a change.

Laurene proposed to the company that she work locally for them on a part-time basis. They were disappointed, but accepted her plan. Once engaged in her artwork again,

Laurene felt renewed and went on to surpass her previous accomplishments and innovations. Anxiety and exhaustion were no longer a problem. They had simply been a messenger telling her to be true to her innate talent. Many of us are visited by this kind of "messenger" when we stray from our talent's natural direction.

Whether you are in a 9-to-5 job, working freelance or have your own business, your talent can be the best career coach you will ever have. Consult with it, and pay close attention to what it tells you.

Talent As Healer and Guide (Part 1)

MATERIALS: Talent Journal and felt pens

Think about a time when you felt anxious, depressed or uncomfortable and you engaged in some activity that helped you feel better. With your dominant hand, write about it in your Talent Journal. Ask yourself:

- What were the circumstances?
- Exactly how did I feel?
- What seemed to be triggering the feelings?
- What did I do that made me feel better?
- What decision did I make?
- What action did I take?

I was getting ready to move. I was leaving a situation with 2 roommates and moving to a place of my own. Things were very tense. I pulled out some paints and painted for a while. It was my own private time. I felt calmer. And more relaxed.

Talent As Healer and Guide (Part 2)

MATERIALS: Talent Journal and felt pens

Anytime you feel anxious, worried or stressed about work, write a dialog with your talent. Ask questions with your dominant hand, let your talent answer with your non-dominant hand. See the talent as a person. For instance, your talent for business appears as the *Business Woman* or *Business Man*; your love for dancing becomes the *Dancer*. (You can also draw a picture of this part of your personality with your non-dominant hand).

Ask the talent's opinion about the following:

- What might be causing my discomfort?
- Is this a sign that you are not expressing in my life?
- Is there anything you can do to help me feel better?
- What do you think would get my life back in balance?

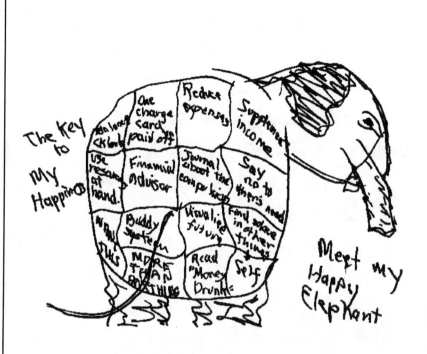

Meet my happy elephant

Why do I overspend? What is causing the problem?

There is a profound sense of longing or need. I think it is about love. Love for self. Being used to judging myself externally rather than internally. Can I find solace in spending

if I can't find it in myself? Time to let go of
the ineffective fix and get back to the God-
given knowledge that I was born with. Sense
of self. Overspending is the same as
stuffing my emotions.

Is there anything you can do to help me feel better?

I will try my best to keep you connected to
the truth about yourself. I can continue to
give you creative ideas for making money
and finding resources to help you. I think the
connection to Self will reduce the craving.

I forgive you for spending too much and
think you have more than enough money to
get yourself out of this jam. Like attracts
like. As you connect to your inner powers,
you will attract all that you need. Visualize
your Happy Elephant.

WORK STYLE AND CAREER

Career means different things to different people. Some define career as a job (or a series of jobs) providing upward mobility such as promotions, additional responsibility, increasing financial rewards, etc. For self-employed individuals, career is often seen as a steadily growing set of skills to market and goals to attain.

People have a wide range of work styles. An individual's style preference plays a key role in the type of jobs he or she selects. With variations, we generally see two basic preferences.

Many people gravitate toward work that involves intense, focused projects. For them, work is a series of project-based, finite assignments with a beginning, middle and end. The entertainment industry is built upon this model. Stage, screen and television productions are planned with one program, film or series in mind. When production is finished, the work is over. The same is true in the aerospace industry, which operates from contract to contract.

Others have more traditional work styles. This is typified by regular working hours (9-to-5), a work station or office, pay increases, incentives, benefits and opportunities for promotion and retirement. Until recently, this work style has given employees security by delivering a regular paycheck and work stability. However, currently this particular style preference is in the greatest state of flux. Although millions are employed at 9-to-5 jobs, the security they sought is now threatened. Those who have lost their positions are facing job searches and may be forced into project-based careers.

What's My Line? (Part 1)

MATERIALS: Talent Journal and felt pens

1. With your dominant hand, ask yourself the following questions about your natural work style:

   - Do I feel more secure working a full-time job?
   - Do I prefer freelance, consulting or individual assignment work?
   - What type of work/job allows my talent to flow most freely?
   - What type of structure or schedule allows my talent to grow?
   - Do I work best alone or in a team?
   - Does my lifestyle support my natural work style? If not, what do I want to do about it?

2. Using your non-dominant hand, draw a picture of yourself in the type of work that would allow your talent to have full expression.

What is my natural work style?

My work style is to perform tasks or work assignments to completion. Unless I have been given limits on the hours I am to work, I will modify these hours by working overtime to complete a task rather than letting it go to the next work period.

My security comes in knowing I have done a job to the best of my ability, whether it be a so-called full-time job or not.

Do I prefer freelance, consulting or individual assignment work?

I prefer consulting, since this falls in the supervising category. Showing, assisting, training and developing good work habits for others to follow.

What type of structure or schedule allows my talent to grow?

When I am told that a goal must be reached, I like to decide what needs to be done and how. This is the philosophy I used when directing the work of others.

Do I work best alone or in a team?

I work best with one other person or on a team. Working alone does not appeal to me, although I have had to do it at times.

Does my lifestyle support my natural work style?

Yes.

What's My Line? (Part 2)

MATERIALS: Talent Journal and felt pens

Project yourself into the future and describe the lifestyle that would support the scene you depicted in the drawing in Part 1. Using your dominant hand, answer the following questions in your Talent Journal:

- Where do you live? Are you living alone or with others?
- Do you travel or not?
- What are you doing for a living? How do you feel about it?
- How much money are you making per year?
- What skills have you developed?
- List some accomplishments.
- Include any other aspects of your ideal work and lifestyle, i.e., hobbies, community activities, etc.

Ideal Lifestyle

I am an independent consultant living in a mountain town in a beautiful log cabin with

water, trees, solitude, pet & soul mate.
Travel to projects, doing some pre-planning
and prep at home.

Rewards are abundant. Working 2 weeks a
month and more than fulfilling my needs.
Walking, teaching exercise, therapeutic
touch, my pets, gardening, cleaning &
puttering are large components.

I am being paid for my creative abilities
to bring a project to fruition & have
success in people's perception that it was
fun & productive. Work as literacy
advocate. Travel to see family at least
every other month.

THE CAREER COLLECTION

For some, career consists of a collection of different jobs. Like
colored beads strung on a necklace, their employment history
appears to be a miscellaneous list of unrelated activities.

Janet had been a bartender, office manager, exercise coach, school bus driver, and multi-level marketing representative. At 31 she is still excited about experiencing more variety. The adage that "variety is the spice of life" describes Janet's "career" in a nutshell.

Janet's conglomeration of jobs would certainly perplex anyone who defines career as a ladder leading to "advancement." Such a person would observe Janet's work history and ask: "What does it all add up to?" Janet's is decidedly a non-linear approach to career. It consists of a broad range of knowledge and information gathered seemingly at random.

Look a little closer, however, and some order does emerge. Janet is exercising a variety of talents. Within this variety you'll definitely see a pattern. The work she has done requires two things: physical energy and communication skills. Janet is active and she's a people person.

This career path is more orderly than it may appear. It is usually based on a core body of talents, knowledge and skills that have been collected over time. The data builds upon itself; one piece of information ties into another and forms unusual relationships. This, incidentally, is one definition of creativity: *Making connections between things that, on the surface, seem unrelated.* When enough information ties together, a purpose often emerges with time. It may not have been clear at the outset, but through the rear-view mirror, a definite pattern or design has been revealed.

In the "jack-of-all-trades" career, the jobs vary in responsibility, financial rewards or social status. It is decidedly a non-linear approach and seems to be particularly popular with Generation X. This is the least understood of all career paths. However, it is turning out to be highly compatible with our current economy. It has *survival* written all over it. Knowing that you can survive is a strong basis for inner security, confidence, flexibility and marketability.

Jobs, Jobs, Jobs (Part 1)

MATERIALS: Talent Journal and felt pens

1. Using your dominant hand, make a list of all the jobs you've ever had. If there are too many to remember, just list as many as you can recall. They do not have to be in chronological order. These may have been full-time employment, part-time work, freelance assignments, projects, etc.

2. Look over your list. What talents and skills do you see expressing in these jobs or projects? Are there any talents that seem to show up in all or most of these jobs? What are they? With your non-dominant hand, list them on another page.

EMPLOYMENT RECORD

- Assistant/ clerk: Shipping, Receiving, Production Assistant
- Assistant/ clerk: Model Building, Architectural Drafting, Shipping and

Receiving, Quarterly Inventory
- Courier
- Lamp Assembler
- Telemarketing—Promotional Rep
- Auto Mechanic
- Automotive Service Installer—Tires, Batteries, Alternators, Generators, etc.
- Production Assistant—Building Systems Mfg.
- Administrative Assistant/ Interior Designer
- Service Writer
- Parts Manager
- Assistant Manager, Auto Service
- Dispatcher—Auto Service
- High-End Audio Technician/ Installer/ Inventory Control
- Membership Director/ Event Coordinator—Vintage Racing Club
- Production Manager—Publishing
- Waitress
- Director of Purchasing—Steel Building Systems
- Researcher—Steel Building Systems

- Administrative Assistant/ Restaurant
- Catering Director
- Editor
- Multimedia Producer
- Contractor—Building Arts

TALENTS AND SKILLS

- Mechanical
- Good organizer
- Good planner
- High energy
- Problem solver
- People skills
- Computer skills
- Production know-how (interactive multimedia/ publishing)
- Communication skills—editing
- Team builder
- Budgeting skills
- Tenacious

Jobs, Jobs, Jobs (Part 2)

MATERIALS: Talent Journal and felt pens

1. Turn to a new page. With your dominant hand, draw a group of circles. Inside each circle write the name of one talent you expressed in your previous jobs. Along with the talent, write down the job function. For example:

   > Talent: good communicator
   > Jobs: selling, managing, coaching
   >
   > Talent: organizing groups
   > Jobs: managing, coaching

2. With your dominant hand, draw a line connecting the circles. The idea is to combine talents and job functions that seem to form a marketable package at this time in your life.

3. With your dominant hand, write about how you might combine these talents in a new way and apply them to needs that others have.

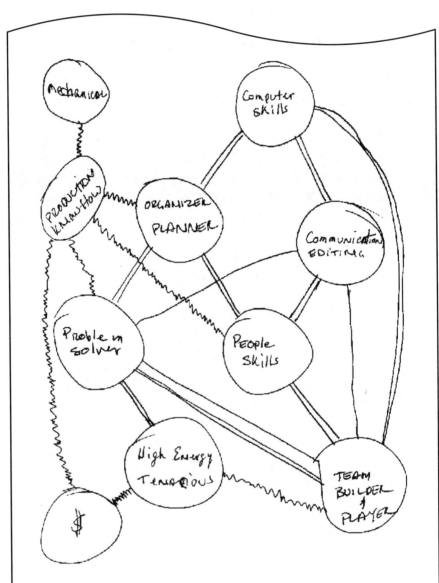

(Squiggly line connecting circles)
- Mechanical
- Production know-how
- Organizer/ planner

- People skills
- Problem solver
- Budget skills $
- High energy/ tenacious
- Team builder/ team player
- Computer skills

I can use all these skills marketing myself as a:

Consultant for Producing Interactive Multimedia Exhibits at Trade Shows or other venues

WORK IS LOVE

Perhaps the simplest but most profound career advice is to be found in one sentence. In his book, *The Prophet*, Kahlil Gibran wrote:

"Work is love made visible."

Finding your own career path is a journey that provides you with precious knowledge about your talents and yourself. It is a self-discovery process that reveals who you are, how you behave and what actions to take. Your talent will lead you to respect and love yourself.

Life is very precious. So is talent. Most of us spend a large percentage of our lives at work. We deserve to *love* the work we do and to express our talents in the process. We deserve what we accept. Once we accept and embrace the idea of loving our work, we can move ahead.

Working with Love (Part 1)

MATERIALS: Talent Journal and felt pens

1. With your dominant hand, write a thank-you letter to someone who, through his or her example, has taught you the value of loving work. This can be a person living or dead.

    - How did this person demonstrate love of work?
    - How did he or she impact your life and your approach to work and career?
    - If it's appropriate, you might send such a letter to this person or anyone else who showed you how to love work.

Dear L:

Thank you for being such an inspiration in helping me to claim myself as an artist and writer. Your resilient spirit & tenacity make me more committed to my dreams than ever. I see you move through hard spots with a no-problem attitude. Your work is a part of you—you glow from it—it gives you energy & strength even though it's hard. I see you share yourself with others so they can see themselves more fully. You see people's talent, gifts, potential. I keep striving to be more creative, since it sets me free.

Blessings, M

Working with Love (Part 2)

MATERIALS: Collage materials

On a sheet of art paper, create a "work is love made visible" photo collage. Picture things you have loved about any work you've ever done, be it paid or volunteer, amateur or professional level.

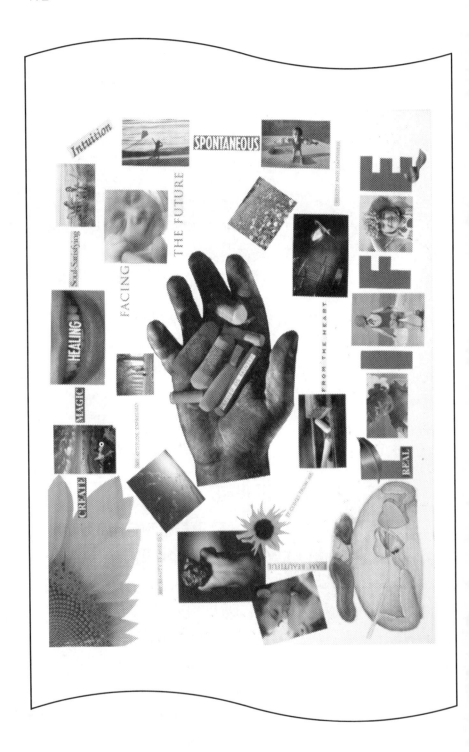

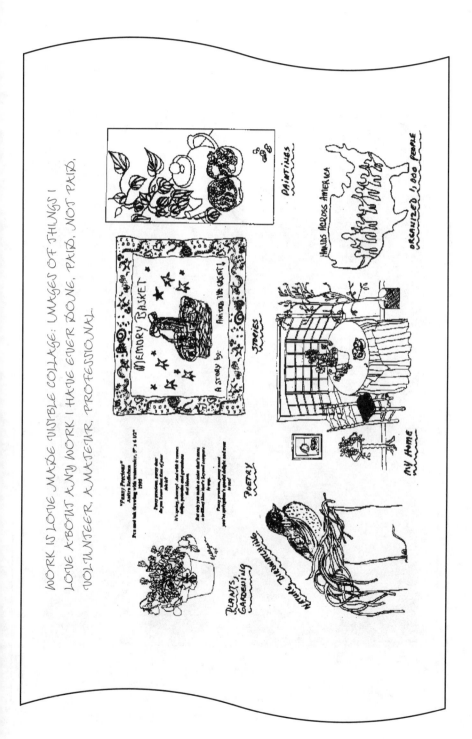

REDEFINING CAREER

It's a good idea to periodically redefine your career. This includes reassessing your lifestyle and talent on a regular basis. Look for symptoms of dissatisfaction, boredom or stress. These symptoms may be a message that it is time to pay attention to your talent. Seek productivity, joy and freedom. Lucia had a personal experience with this kind of self-inventory a number of years ago when she went into high gear as an author.

My first published book had been out for a few years. In the meantime, I was working on some other books. One day I asked myself, *What will it take to redirect my energy and resources to get these books published?*

I assessed the situation and discovered that I was spending too much time supporting an expensive lifestyle. I would need to devote a lot more time to the business of getting published. How could I do this? Cut down on my expenses by moving into a smaller, less expensive place; raise some cash by selling furniture and other items I wouldn't need if I had less space to furnish; devote more time to writing and editing and less to generating income. With fewer expenditures and more time, I could do it.

I chose to live a rather Spartan life for a few years, but it freed me up to write, publish and then travel doing book promotion. It was well worth it. The five-year period that followed was one of the most joyful and productive of my life and afforded me a freedom I had never known.

Recently, reassessment has been forced on many people. Corporations are offering early retirement packages to reduce staff and cut costs. Having to decide whether to take advantage of these offers has made people reconsider their careers. Many who have taken advantage of these packages are not retiring but are entering work in another field.

An aerospace company was downsizing. In an effort to get rid of the less productive employees, they offered early retirement. Much to their surprise, it was the top talent that opted for retirement. The company did an interview survey of those who left. During the interviews, they discovered that many had seriously thought through what was really important to them. They realized that they had stopped enjoying their work a long time ago and felt their jobs had become routine. All of them took pride in the quality of their performance but had begun to yearn for something more.

Many individuals see the handwriting on the wall. Instead of *waiting* for layoffs or early retirement, they plan for it; some even develop businesses on the side.

> Raoul and his wife, Luisa, both worked for an electronics manufacturing firm. They operated an antiques business on the weekends. This offered Raoul an opportunity to refinish old furniture, which he enjoyed tremendously. He loved seeing old, forgotten things come back to life. It also gave Luisa a chance to put her natural talent for sales to good use.

> When the electronics company relocated to another state, they offered early retirement packages to qualifying employees. The couple decided not to pull up stakes and move. They chose early retirement instead. With less income and fewer benefits, Raoul and Luisa had to make some changes. They would not have as much money to travel as they had before. They had to scrap their plans to add an extra room to their home. On the other hand, they had more time to devote to their antiques business. They also had more time for each other, friends, family and especially their grandchildren. In the long run, the trade-offs were minimal and the reward was a quality of life that was far superior to what they had known. They felt it was definitely worth it.

If the Truth Be Told

MATERIALS: Talent Journal and felt pens

1. Think about a career or job you would really love to have. In your Talent Journal, with your dominant hand, complete the following sentences:
   If the truth be told, I would _____.
   What is holding me back is _____.
   If I wanted to, I could _____.
   If I had the courage, I would _____.
   What I need is _____.
   When I'm ready, I will _____.

2. If you had enough money to retire today, what would you do? Write about it in your Talent Journal.

If the truth be told, I would be a co-author of books, helping people who can't write but have great information. I would assist them to research their material and express their ideas.

What is holding me back is that I don't yet have enough experience in the publishing industry or a name for myself as a writer.

If I wanted to, I could contact someone who wants to write a book but doesn't know how.

If I had the courage, I would start making calls and setting up deals with publishers.

What I need is a co-author and a publishing contract.

When I'm ready, I will go for it!

> If I had enough money and could "retire" today, I would travel, do photography, artwork, write fiction and travel stories and books.

Action

Identify some people you know who have very different career styles. Here are some possibilities:

- An employee in a traditional 9-to-5 job.
- A person who works at home.
- A person carrying two or three jobs simultaneously.
- An entrepreneur with his or her own business.
- An individual working in seasonal jobs, e.g., construction in good weather and computer work in bad weather.
- A jack-of-all-trades with a broad variety of projects and jobs.
- A person who travels as his or her job.

Conduct an interview with two or three of these individuals. At the interview, ask the following questions:

- How did you decide on your career style?
- Did you prepare for it by going to school, getting training, etc.?

- What reward do you get from your career style?
- How do you measure your success?
- Why and how does this career style work for you?
- Of what significance is the location or environment in which you work?

Talent Workout

Heart's Desire
Have you been developing the habit of asking about your **heart's desire** regarding your everyday life?

Talent Review
Have you been making and keeping **regular appointments** devoted to your talent? Have you been keeping your Talent Journal on any regular basis (weekly, daily)?

Feedback
Do a feedback session in your Talent Journal. Ask yourself the following questions:

- What am I learning about my talent?
- What have I been doing for my talent?
- What do I want to do for my talent?
- What have I learned about myself?
- What have I learned about the way I behave?
- What action do I want to take at this time?

CHAPTER SIX

BEING RESPONSIBLE FOR TALENT

ORDER AND CHAOS

Order allows us to function. Without order, chaos prevails. The rules that we live by, as individuals and groups, create order in our lives and guide our actions. Everyone needs some kind of order in his or her life; but the definition of order may vary widely from one individual to the next. Society relies on structure: customs, mores and traditions. When humans form groups, they create rules for maintaining "law and order." In families and households there are usually ground rules regarding who does what and what goes where. Family conflict often plays itself out at these levels. "You didn't throw out the trash. How come you didn't wash the car? Why wasn't this bill paid? That's *your* job." When there is harmony in a family, everyone is pulling his or her weight and sharing responsibilities. No one feels put upon or burdened. Family members know what is expected of them and they cooperate willingly. If problems arise, they communicate and work together toward a solution.

In communities and organizations, order is structured through local and federal law, customs, tradition, policies and procedures. This is true in civic life as well as business, sports, the arts, religion and all areas of human activity. When musicians play together, they read the same music or follow a common tune. Even jazz musicians improvise upon the same agreed-upon melody, chord pattern and key.

In today's socioeconomic climate, many of the old rules simply aren't working. Our environment and our lives are often thrown into chaos. This is especially true in the area of work. We endure cutbacks in government and corporate enterprises and American industry moving toward cheaper foreign labor forces. These things spell insecurity for wage-earners across the board.

This situation has affected all of us. With unemployment on the rise, there is less money in circulation. Everyone suffers, with few exceptions. Add to this an increase of disasters in recent years, such as floods, earthquakes, hurricanes and terrorist bombings. It's easy to understand why many people feel they are living in a world of chaos.

As the world has become more chaotic, scientists are intensifying their studies of chaos dynamics. Recent research in this field suggests that just as order and structure are necessary, so is chaos. Our friend Dr. Valerie Hunt, scientist *extraordinaire* and author of *Infinite Mind: The Science of Human Vibrations*, has pointed out that chaos is a natural state of being. Chaos, according to the theoreticians, is described as multiple orders with the capability to reproduce themselves (in similar structures). In other words, chaos is now perceived as having order in it. Out of chaos, new order and structure emerge.

When we can't *see* order in chaos, we may fall into a psychological abyss. It is common for people faced with catastrophe to go into shock. They simply can't *comprehend* what has happened. They may become non-functional, numb or depressed, or may behave impulsively. Often they become incapable of making decisions or managing their lives responsibly. Lucia has consulted many individuals suffering from these chaos-induced symptoms. Such clients come into therapy because some event has thrown their very existence into question. Their old lives, security and well-being have suddenly been taken away. A home has been destroyed by a natural calamity, a spouse has suddenly walked out or a "secure" job has been eliminated in an instant.

These kinds of events often trigger one of two extreme responses: hysteria or a near-catatonic state. In either case, people are reacting to what they perceive as chaos (an absence of order or predictability). People in the grips of chaos used to be described as having a "nervous breakdown." Today, some people refer to it as "experiencing a paradigm shift," a fancy term for having the rug pulled out from under you.

What's really happening is that the old, familiar order has broken down and the new one hasn't shown its face yet. The "chaotic" situation is a wake-up call, a signal for change. Chaos delivers an invitation: take the pieces of your shattered past and reconfigure them in a whole new pattern. The image of a kaleidoscope comes to mind. As we turn it, pieces of glass fall into ever-changing new designs. If we don't turn it, the pattern stays frozen in place. There's an old saying that describes the challenge of chaos beautifully: "If you want to make an omelet, you have to break some eggs."

Chaos can bring change and revitalization. This new definition invites us to embrace the chaos inherent in crisis and to see it as the ushering in of a period of transition. Transitions are characterized by confusion and lack of structure; they are often unpredictable and scary. A transition is like crossing a river on foot. We're not there yet. We're standing knee-deep in cold water, or hopping rocks and avoiding fallen tree branches. It's uncomfortable and may be very frightening, but it's the only way to get to the other side.

People in transition—divorce, layoff, relocation, convalescence from illness and so on—often describe themselves as confused, scared and challenged. They say things like, "I don't know what I'm doing. It's all so confusing. My life is total chaos. I'm terrified. There aren't any road maps. I don't know what to do." In other words, there aren't any rules for dealing with the crisis, no ready-made guidelines for comprehending it.

In her first book, *The Creative Journal*, Lucia shared a personal journal entry on the subject of chaos. Although struggling with a life-threatening illness and contemplating a career change, she knew intuitively that this was a valuable time. She drew a picture of chaos and then wrote a poem about it.

Treasure the chaos out of which order emerges
Cherish the puzzlement leading to the light
Deep inside this nest is the self to be found
with no road maps to foretell the path
Only a rear-view mirror and a knitting
needle or two
shaped like
pens + pencils

Treasure the chaos
out of which order emerges.
Cherish the puzzlement
leading to the light.
Deep inside this nest is
the Self to be found.

There is a way to restructure our lives out of chaos. We do it by developing the skill of recognizing patterns and making choices. We learn to discover order where there appears to be none. We do this by using our own individual set of values for reorganizing our lives. We examine what is important to us and set new priorities. As new patterns emerge, a foundation of strength can build. We must have patience and faith in the process and ride through the discomfort of "not knowing what we're doing."

German poet Rainer Maria Rilke wrote eloquently about transitions in his book, *Letters to a Young Poet.*

> Be patient toward all that is unsolved in your heart and try to love the questions themselves like locked rooms and like books that are written in a very foreign tongue. . . . And the point is, to live everything. Live the questions now. Perhaps you will then gradually, without noticing it, live along some distant day into the answer.

Aleta's story in Chapter 3 of the Northridge earthquake is a good example of crisis becoming a talent opportunity. However, her quake experience also illustrates perfectly how new order emerges from chaos.

Waking suddenly in total darkness (because all the power had failed), she said, "It felt as if the house had been put in a blender and set on high." The sound of things crashing and breaking all around was terrifying enough, but the fact that no one could see what was going on added to the bedlam.

Needless to say, the entire family was traumatized. They reacted with a full range of emotions, from hysteria to paralysis. There was a period of dazed confusion. "What happened? Was that the 'big one'? How serious is it? How widespread is it? What about family members in other parts of town?" Then there were months of after-shocks to contend with, which kept everyone on edge.

After a period of homelessness and camping out with relatives, the damage was fully assessed and they decided to rebuild. As emergency measures were put in place, the family moved into a rental home provided by the Federal Emergency Management Administration (FEMA). From this base they could embark on the complicated process of tearing down and rebuilding. In other words, a new structure to their lives was taking shape.

For the next 18 months, their lives revolved around a clear series of tasks, schedules and deadlines. It was an intensely productive period, far more so than they had ever known. Although stressful, it was highly structured and completely goal-oriented. Designing and building their new home was by far the biggest accomplishment of their lives. The house itself, much larger than the old dwelling, allows for a whole new way of being. There's more and better planned space for work and play and social interaction for the entire family.

When thinking about chaos, keep in mind: *outer* events that shake us up can bring about *internal* changes in our beliefs and behavior. Call it growth, transformation, a paradigm shift or whatever you like. It all adds up to changing the rules.

THE RULES WE LIVE BY

We've been taught to play by the rules. Our teachers are society, family and personal experience. Early on we learned there were consequences when we disobeyed the rules or broke the law. We found out that children get punished with scoldings, spankings or demerits, or by being sent to their room. Adults get fired, fined or put in jail. Certainly, everybody bends the rules from time to time—driving over the speed limit, telling little white lies and so forth. On the whole, most of us fall into the category of rule-keepers. We generally do not move out of this role unless it is absolutely necessary. After all, sticking to the rules makes life simpler and more manageable, more predictable.

What happens when society's rules suddenly change? What happens when life kicks us in the pants and throws us out of the safe confines of the well-worn groove? This is the predicament that many face regarding their careers. Socioeconomic changes are standing people on their heads, pulling the rug out from under their expectations, plans and dreams for the future.

Let's face it. The rules about employment that we have relied upon for generations no longer apply. We need to search for a new way to approach both career and retirement. For if the old career model doesn't work anymore, neither does the old idea of retirement. Remember, retirement benefits were always tied to the so-called "ladder of success." You worked for a certain number of years, climbed the ladder, got advancements and periodic raises, received your gold watch or a going-away party and retired with a "guaranteed annual income." What happens when employers don't play by those rules anymore, for whatever reason? Chaos sets in. Using talent as a foundation for making career decisions and work choices puts us in charge of our lives.

As the life span extends, the lines between career and retirement are blurring. Some people must supplement their retirement income with part-time jobs. What do we call this? A post-retirement career? What about people engaged in volunteer work? They may be using all their talents to benefit the community as much as they did when they were in the work force. What do we call this? A post-retirement vocation? What about the individuals who go back to work at an age when most people are thinking about retirement?

Order Out of Chaos (Part 1)

MATERIALS: Talent Journal and felt pens

Recall a time when your normal routine or the very structure of your life was dramatically changed by some event. Perhaps this has happened to you many times. Just focus on one of these life-altering situations. Maybe it was a divorce or loss of a loved one, an illness, job loss or some natural disaster. With your dominant hand, write about it in your Talent Journal:

- What happened?
- How did you feel?
- Exactly how did your life change?
- What did you do about it?
- What decisions did you make?
- What actions did you take?
- In retrospect, how did this experience affect you: your attitudes, character, skills, etc?

Several years ago, I was laid off from my job. I was shocked, scared—I was in a panic. I had no savings and a lot of bills! The company I had worked for offered me some freelance work, which I accepted. The result was that I was able to work at home while I looked for a job.

I learned a lot about myself during that time. I was able to cope with not having a regular job with a steady paycheck. I learned that I could rely on myself. That in the worst of financial situations, I could take care of myself.

Order Out of Chaos (Part 2)

MATERIALS: Talent Journal and felt pens

With your non-dominant hand, draw three pictures of the event described in Part 1. Draw them as a cartoon strip from left to right (see next page). Label one frame "before," the second "chaos," and the third "after."

In your first frame, draw an image or symbol for the pattern of your life before the event.

In the second frame, "chaos," show the chaotic part, the transition during which you didn't know which end was up or you were confused or struggling to find order.

In the third frame, draw a picture of the new structure that grew out of the chaos.

Remember, this drawing can be done in symbols or simple abstract lines and shapes. It does not have to be a representational picture.

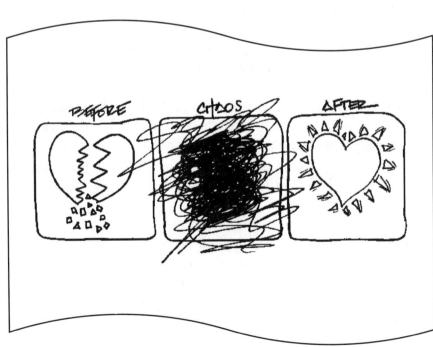

RULES AND CHOICES

It is everyone's responsibility to put his or her own talent to work. When we do, talent becomes the gift that goes on giving (to ourselves and others). Working our talent is easy to do when it falls within the rules that we normally follow. An actor in a successful play shows up at the theater every night and performs his role. He works his talent, gets paid for it and has a sense of security and fulfillment. There is a schedule and structure inherent in his work and the expression of his talent.

It is more challenging when we have to create a new set of rules and operate outside our comfort zone. A nurse who wants to start her own business as a caterer will have to create a whole new set of procedures and rules than the ones to which she is accustomed. As a businesswoman, she must deal with setting prices, negotiating with clients, ordering decorations, preparing food, etc. These are not structures to which nurses are accustomed.

Knowing when to implement rule-keeping or choice-making is a valuable skill. The first step is to determine if a particular task is routine or an exception. Routine tasks can be handled virtually the same way every time. Computers and automation are the "experts" at performing routine tasks. Creativity is required when doing tasks that are exceptions to the rule. When tackling exceptional tasks, we usually learn something new or solve a problem we've never faced. Once we identify the routine tasks, we can automate them. In this way we become more efficient and free ourselves up for the more important things in life.

This principle applies to working our talent. To behave responsibly toward our talent (and our careers), we must know how to handle routine and identify the exceptions. The following story demonstrates what happens when the solution to an exceptional situation is inappropriately turned into a routine:

Maggie was preparing a pot roast for dinner. Before putting it in the pan, she sliced the end off the roast. Her husband, Ken, asked her why she did that, and Maggie replied, "Oh, that's the way my mother always did it. I don't really know why. She must have had a reason." The next time the couple ate at Maggie's mother's home, Ken asked his mother-in-law why she sliced the end off her pot roast. The reply: "Oh, my good pot roast pan was never big enough for the size roast I needed to feed this crowd, so I had to cut off the end of the roast."

An example of someone who questioned rules and routine was Malcolm, a toy designer. As you will see from his story, his ability to deal creatively with standard ways of doing things led to a personal win as well as a success for his employer.

When he started working for a major toy manufacturer, Malcolm noticed that the company's field-testing was conducted in sterile, isolated testing rooms. It appeared to Malcolm that this was an artificial process and did not take into account what children really liked and how they played in real life. However, sales were good, so he figured the company must know something he didn't about the customers who paid for the items.

As the market changed and competition increased, the company started to falter. The toy designers were constantly pressured by management to explore every toy idea imaginable so they could beat out competitors. In this stressful environment, there was a nervous flurry of new designs but sales did not pick up. The company continued to field-test and make its market decisions in the same old manner.

The more he analyzed the situation, the more strongly Malcolm felt that the best toys would not be forthcoming unless they changed their testing procedures. He wrote proposals and talked to management about his previous experiences field-testing in the community with children in their "natural habitat," as he put it. No one seemed to understand. Mostly, they were paranoid about the theft of product ideas by spies from other companies. (Their fear did have some basis in reality, as there is a fair amount of espionage and blatant imitations—called "knock-offs"—in the toy industry.)

Malcolm felt responsible to both his talent and his company. He knew he would have to take a different course of action. On his own time, Malcolm arranged to have the toys tested, under confidential conditions in houses, classrooms and day-care centers in his community. Malcolm then had to run his designs through the in-house evaluation procedures. The toys that were popular with children in classrooms and homes also proved to be a hit in the sterile toy-testing room at the company's headquarters. Malcolm's toys made it to the marketplace and were big sellers.

Off the Beaten Path

MATERIALS: Talent Journal and felt pens

1. Have you ever solved a problem creatively by following the guidance of your own intuition, judgment or experience? With your dominant hand, write about it in your Talent Journal.

   - Have you ever faced rigid rules or outworn procedures?
   - What was the situation?
   - Who were the people who were set in their ways?
   - What were the rules (conscious or unconscious)?
   - How did you deal with people? With the rules?
   - What was the result?

2. Are you faced with any situations today where outworn policies, procedures or rules are

hampering your creativity or the full expression of your talent? With your dominant hand, draw a picture of the situation. With your non-dominant hand, make another drawing showing the problem solved.

When I was a Head Start director the government gave us a materials budget. I reviewed it. I went to my supervisor and told her that the absurdly low figure was unworkable. I told her that I'd probably resign because there was no way we could do a good job with this budget. She understood my frustration.

We went to our agency's accountant and explained our dilemma. He asked us, "Where's the fat in this budget?" I replied: "There's too much money in administration that I'd rather put into classroom equipment." We reallocated funds from one budget category to another. He explained that it wouldn't cost a penny more. We got what we needed and we did a good job.

I was working on my bachelor's degree in business. I wasn't sure if business was the area I wanted to be in. My friends said: "Stay in school, you're so close to finishing." I felt that if I didn't finish, I was a flake who couldn't make up my mind.

I decided to take time off from school. I took some adult education classes and am doing volunteer work in order to get clearer on what I want to do.

I was able to articulate to friends why I needed to take a break. Some understood and gave their support while others just didn't get it. I've learned to live my life on my own terms—and follow what I feel to be right for me. If you follow someone else's rules, you end up living someone else's life.

CHANGING RULES

When we create rules, we often assume that they will last forever. This is especially true if we have had success playing by the rules. It is very difficult to give up rules that have served us well, that may have once supported us but are now a hindrance. Many rules have been inherited from family members, mentors or loved ones and we may feel strangely disloyal if we change, break or abandon these outworn rules. It's as if we are letting those people down.

Rules reflect beliefs and attitudes, and these do not die easily. It is important to make sure that rules serve talent. Many people make the mistake of allowing rules to become more important than talent. When this happens, they are no longer connected to their talent; instead, they are being run by their rules.

Josh was an experienced manager who had been through three layoffs. The first one was caused by a merger, resulting in a duplication of managerial staff. In looking around for another position, Josh felt confident about his previous track record and was shooting for a comparable position in another company. He settled into what he thought would be a secure job with a future.

No such luck. Within a year and a half he was told that management positions were being consolidated. "You could stay for six months," he was told, but he chose a voluntary layoff. Four months later he landed another job. The new firm turned out to be highly unstable. Its parent company was going bankrupt. Josh was told that he could ride it out, but obviously there could be no promise of continued employment. He elected to hang in there. Finally, he was laid off.

Josh felt demoralized and depressed. There were fewer positions available, and he was competing with younger men and women with less experience who were described as "cheap, energetic risk-takers." All of this left him emotionally depleted and financially stretched to the limit. Things were complicated by Josh's unwillingness to diversify, to try smaller companies, to take less money or to move out of management altogether. He tried to duplicate the same position with every firm he worked for. It took Josh 18 months to find a job with a smaller firm that had just restructured itself to stay in business.

Josh had spent five years looking for a secure job. During all that time he clung to the rules he knew, thinking that they would continue working for him. His rules were: *One should steadily advance in his career. Larger, well known companies are better. Pay cuts spell disaster and signal failure. Changes or loss of job status are embarrassing and indicate that one has been derailed from the success track.*

These rules were so ingrained that he simply had no awareness that they no longer worked for him. If he had listened to his talent, he might have been guided in a different direction. Josh thought the road to success was paved with rules instead of his talent. Had he delved deeper into himself, he might have turned crisis into an opportunity. The career map he had created wasn't working. If Josh had seen it as a sign that he needed to draw a new map, his career might have been completely revitalized.

Rules of the Road

MATERIALS: Talent Journal and felt pens

1. What are your rules about talent, career, success? With your dominant hand, complete the following sentences:

   - My talent could _____.
   - I know I am successful in my career when _____.

   - In order to have a fulfilling career, I must _____.

   - I was successful when I_____.
   - I will be successful if I_____.

2. Reflect upon your family's attitude toward talent, career and success. What rules did they live by regarding these subjects? With your dominant hand, write about it in your journal.

   Re-read your answers to #1. Is there any connection between your family's rules and yours? If so, what is it? Are you happy with your current rules or are there some you would like to change? If so, which ones would you change? What would you change them to?

- My talent could guide my career.
- I know I am successful in my career when my talent is expressing and I'm being paid well for it.
- In order to have a fulfilling career, I must do what I enjoy doing most.
- I was successful when I followed my heart.
- I will be successful if I have faith.

My family's attitude toward career and success consists of getting a good job (i.e., secure and pays well) and making

sure you keep it. Long-term employment
is the key to success. Talent is okay for
hobbies and free time—but not as a career
choice—particularly if it doesn't pay well.

BELIEFS, RULES AND CHOICES

It is important to know how these external rules affect our lives. However, it is equally important that we be aware of our *internally* based rules, the expectations and demands we place on ourselves and others. These are the informal rules. Often they are not clearly defined. They may even be totally unconscious. These personal rules reflect our values and belief system.

Beliefs are originally handed down to us by family and society. However, some of our beliefs change, to one degree or another, in response to our own unique experiences. Our beliefs change and our behaviors change. To caretake our talent, we need to know about our own informal rules and the informal rules of others. These rules will have a profound influence on our talent development. They affect our behavior and the way we view opportunity.

Mapping the Road, Creating the Rules

MATERIALS: Talent Journal and felt pens

1. With your non-dominant hand, draw a map of where you want to be with your talent in one year, five years or ten years. You choose the time frame. Show the road to get there, indicate who can help and who might hinder your growth.

2. With your dominant hand, write the new rules you want to use in achieving your goal. What are your values? How do you want to play the game of talent, career and life?

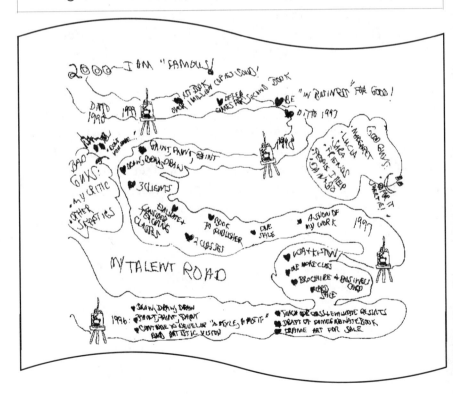

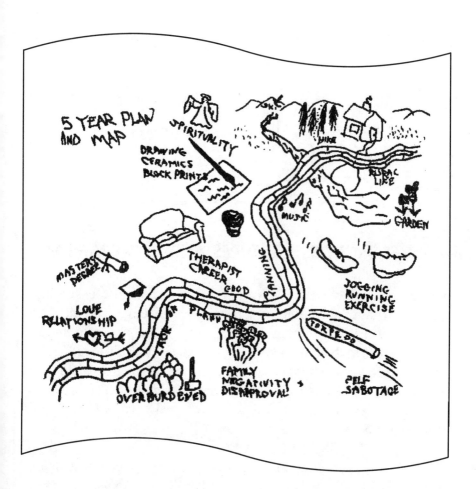

- What you can visualize you can realize.
- Life isn't difficult if you're willing to listen and trust yourself (your spirit).
- Presenting a clean, clear you inside and out will attract the same to you.

- Living in your heart, you'll live in your truth.
- Youth is maintained by living your truth, in your heart. It's so much easier.

RULES ACROSS CULTURES AND GENERATIONS

When we work within a given set of rules, we are essentially working within the confines of a puzzle. The pieces are all there and the task consists of ordering them correctly. If the process is simple, we feel comfortable. We like things to match and fit together. We are uncomfortable when pieces appear to be missing or when there are too many for us to deal with. When things don't match or fit, our rules are tested. When this happens, we usually say, "This doesn't make sense."

Our own rules get tested in a big way when we are confronted with people, customs or beliefs that are different from our own. These situations invite us to accept the differences. This is usually called *tolerance*. However, we prefer the term *acceptance* because tolerance has so many negative connotations, such as "putting up with," bearing, enduring, suffering, etc. Accepting differences does not require that we be converted to or agree with others who believe or behave differently than we do. Acceptance simply opens us to considering other options from which to choose.

As we all know, this is not easy. If "the other" person is foreign or holds beliefs that are in conflict with ours, the tendency is to hold fast to our own beliefs and opinions, to disagree and to criticize the other for being "wrong." That makes us "right," of course. So we get into a battle of good vs. bad, superiority vs. inferiority. Naturally, we're going to put ourselves on the side of "right." This is the basis of all prejudice.

When faced with the foreign or "the different," we think that by accepting others we have to renounce ourselves. This is clearly not true. When we *accept*, we express mutual respect; we live and let live.

At 45, Glenn was the president of a multi-million-dollar distribution firm. A very astute businessman, he was also genuinely concerned about the well-being of his employees. One day, two of Glenn's favorite up-and-coming employees resigned. He was perplexed and called Peggy for a consultation. Glenn explained that both men were in their early 20s and held good positions in the company. He was quite surprised at their resignation because both of their futures with the company had looked so bright.

Glenn told Peggy, "They resigned for ridiculous reasons. One guy even said we didn't have a baseball team and that really bothered him. The other one said he was disappointed when his best friend and co-worker was transferred to another facility and they could no longer work together." Neither reason made any sense at all to Glenn.

Peggy offered to speak with both employees. After doing so, she understood why the resignations were confounding Glenn. These two young men came from a generation that has a different set of values and rules. Their perspective of time and relationships are different from Glenn's. These employees are not striving for upward mobility in one company. Rather, they see work as an opportunity for developing relationships and receiving a salary. At the same time, they are both conscientious and perform their work very well. That is why Glenn was grooming them to climb the "ladder of success" within his company.

These young men did not come to work early and leave late, as Glenn's generation of ambitious employees did.

Instead, they arrived on time and left when the official work day was over. They valued life and relationships outside the job. Furthermore, they were very comfortable with their personal rules and expectations about work and career. Glenn was also comfortable about his beliefs regarding what work and a successful career should be.

When Glenn learned about these two employees' job and career rules, he was startled. He saw the loss of these valuable men as senseless. He sat down and negotiated with them so that everyone's needs could be met. They came to a workable solution and the two men decided to stay. Glenn is now more sensitive to the needs of his younger employees. He knows that he will increasingly have to rely on workers from this age group. He realizes that he has to integrate their values into his company's culture and create rules that work for everyone. It is to Glenn's credit that he was flexible enough to change and smart enough to know the cost if he didn't.

Everyone knows that differences such as religion, race, culture and gender spark the most conflict in society. We are all prisoners of our own unconscious rules. When someone else plays by rules that are far different from ours, we have to take a second look at our values and beliefs. That's why many people make it a policy to never discuss politics or religion; they simply don't want to get into conflict. In trying to stay in the comfort zone, many of us seek job opportunities that bolster our own values, standards and rules. Sometimes we have to examine the limitations of our rules, as Glenn did. This is especially true if our old rules are keeping us from reaching our new goals. We may just have to abandon or adapt some of our rules to serve our talent and our career.

Peggy worked with a young woman who was learning how unspoken rules impact behavior.

Tiffany was a highly creative, very outspoken woman. She managed a research and design team within a corporation. Her staff, called the Product Team, was responsible for developing all the new consumer products for the firm. Tiffany's team was extremely productive and had received recognition by upper management. On the other hand, Tiffany herself was not popular with upper management and this left her puzzled. She saw herself as honest, straightforward and innovative. She also knew the importance of balancing people, time and budgets on her projects. *What else could the company want of her?* she wondered. She was pleased that her team received praise. However, she felt slighted when she was passed over for a promotion and raise.

We started exploring the problem. I asked Tiffany about the spoken and unspoken rules of the company. She seemed clear about their official statements (spoken rules) but not about the company's unspoken rules. It hadn't occurred to her to even consider this dimension of the "playing field." I pointed out to her that each company's culture has its own unwritten rules that employees are expected to follow. She had no idea how to find out about these.

I told Tiffany that it wasn't easy. The group often lets new members figure things out on their own. Sometimes someone will take on the role of a mentor and initiate the novice into the way the group operates. Tiffany did not have a mentor. It was assumed that she knew the group behavior and would act accordingly. I suggested she carefully observe body language and other clues to see if she might be out of step in certain situations.

Back at work, Tiffany started observing closely. What she discovered was that speaking out about management problems in a group situation with upper management was taboo. However, if it was done in private where no one "looked bad," it was okay. Tiffany realized that her directness and honesty were in conflict with an unspoken rule she had been breaking unwittingly. She also noticed that in small conferences, everyone took their turn in the order they were seated around the table. They never spoke out of turn, especially the women. Tiffany realized that she had broken this unspoken rule. It became clear that, although she performed well at her job, she was being judged for breaking the informal rules. In the eyes of management she had been labeled as "difficult." She decided to communicate more thoughtfully and strategically. After a few months, Tiffany reported that she was finally getting the raise and promotion she had wanted and that managers had accepted her fully.

At one time or another, everyone falls prey to the unspoken rules of a group. The more conscious we are about these informal rules, the easier it is for us to recognize them and choose a course of action.

Generation Gaps and Cultural Divides

MATERIALS: Talent Journal and felt pens

With your dominant hand, write about a time when your talents, dreams or personal decisions were hampered by a conflict with someone of another generation, gender or ethnic/cultural group.

- Whom was the conflict with?
- What happened?
- How did you feel?
- What did you do?

In the early 80s, I was office manager for a well-known architect. Having to manage copious amounts of data, I suggested we buy a computer. "What a great idea!" my boss said. I called all my "hacker" friends and found a good package deal on a used computer, printer and software.

We bought the machine and had it delivered. I was very enthusiastic to finally get the equipment in and knew we'd save a lot of time and money. There was only one problem. Every time I sat down to start using it, my boss would interfere and find something else for me to do. These were invariably trivial tasks, like sorting through old junk mail. After a week of these distractions, I made no progress on the computer. My boss finally said, "I'd rather you not use the computer until I've figured it out."

Weeks rolled by and my frustration mounted. Finally I realized that this computer was destined to collect dust. It became clear that my boss was computer-phobic. I worked there for several more months and the computer sat in the corner—unused. It was quite disappointing, so I left and got a position managing a small desktop publishing firm where I was finally able to use my computer skills.

CREATIVITY BETWEEN THE RULES

It is our belief that creativity happens between the rules. This simply means that the space between the rules is a creative space. Anyone who has ever edited hard copy knows that the space between lines is the place for making changes. It is the space for being creative to improve the final product. The space between the rules can be risky territory. It is often typified as chaotic, ambiguous and uncertain. We might succeed gloriously or fail miserably.

In a business organization, the space between the rules can be marked by change or growth. Such progress can be found in restructuring or in research and development of new products or services. The space between the rules can be seen as an open field for creativity and talent to flourish or as a disaster zone. Talent grows in the soil of creativity, so we need to spend time between the rules to develop our talent. Remember, rules can be a trap, but if we can play *around* them, they can free us. Jazz musicians know this. They start with a chord pattern and melody. From there they jump into the space between and improvise. This principle also applies when creating a career path.

An engineer by the name of Ron left a large corporation because he felt burdened with paperwork, top-heavy management and outdated policies and procedures. In Ron's view, these cumbersome structures killed creativity and fostered inefficiency. The corporate culture had become too confining for him.

Ron began his own business in a home office with a computer link-up to his network of contacts. From this base of operations he was able to market himself and deliver most of the trouble-shooting services he was offering to his clients. To save money, he decided to do most of the tasks himself, including drafting, correspondence, invoicing and bookkeeping. When necessary, he subcontracted other talent on an as-needed basis, keeping his overhead low.

Ron's approach was driven by the nature of his projects. A set of rules seemed to evolve organically out of each particular project and client relationship. When working with his subcontractors, Ron helped them figure out which procedure was best for the project. Ron and his team were essentially problem-solving between the rules. They stayed flexible and always on the cutting edge, watching for new challenges. Today, they are sought after by large construction, entertainment and leisure development firms because of their creativity and inventiveness. They have a reputation for getting the job done, no matter how difficult it is.

RULES IN TIMES OF CRISIS

Our personal rules govern our actions. Under stress, we usually resort to behavior that is familiar and comfortable. We follow our habitual internal rule structure. This behavior is based on who we think we are and how we express in the world. So if you're not sure which rules you live by, observe yourself under pressure or in stress. In creating a career path, it is most important to understand that our personal rules shape our actions. It is our responsibility to create rules for ourselves that foster talent and guide our career.

Crisis and Change

MATERIALS: Talent Journal and felt pens

1. Go back to Chapter One, and review the exercise titled *Turning Crisis into Opportunity.* If you did the exercise in your Talent Journal, re-read it now.

2. On a new page in your journal, with your dominant hand, make three columns. Column 1 is labeled "Crisis." Column 2 is labeled "Action." Column 3 is labeled "Rule."

   • In column 1, with your dominant hand, list the major crises you have faced in your life. Write them in chronological order.

   • In column 2, with your dominant hand, write the action you took in relation to the crisis.

   • In column 3, with your dominant hand, write down the personal rule of behavior that was revealed by your action.

3. Are you facing a crisis in your life at this time? If so, write about it. What action would you normally take? Does that feel appropriate or effective to you? If not, can you consider a different action? What do you think the results would be? Write about it.

CRISIS	ACTION	RULE
WAS ADOPTED	WITHDREW EMOTIONALLY ANGRY	DON'T TRUST MANY PEOPLE
ADOPTED MOTHER DIED	STRONG FOR REST OF FAMILY	PEOPLE YOU TRUST LEAVE.
LEFT FIANCÉ/MOVED TO ANOTHER STATE	MOVED - STARTED OVER	BELIEVE IN YOUR-SELF
LOST JOB	LOOKED FOR NEW JOB- FREELANCED	I CAN TAKE CARE OF MYSELF.
FOUND BIRTH FAMILY BIRTH MOTHER HAD ALREADY DIED.	GOT TO KNOW HER THROUGH OTHER FAMILY MEMBERS.	MY BIRTH MOTHER LOVED ME.

ACTION

Write out an action plan for developing your talent by answering the following questions:

- What talent(s) have I identified to be developed?
- What steps have I already taken to develop this talent?
- Am I satisfied with the action that I have taken in developing the talent?
- What do I plan to do now in order to further develop this talent?

- What is my one-year projection in relationship to this talent?
- What is my five-year projection in relationship to this talent?
- What is the next step I need to take toward my one-year projection?
- When will I take this next step?

Talent Workout

Heart's Desire
Have you been developing the habit of asking about your heart's desire regarding your everyday life?

Talent Review
Have you been making and keeping regular appointments devoted to your talent? Have you been keeping your Talent Journal on any regular basis (weekly, daily)?

Feedback
Do a feedback session in your Talent Journal. Ask yourself the following questions:

- What am I learning about my talent?
- What have I been doing for my talent?
- What do I want to do for my talent?
- What have I learned about myself?
- What have I learned about the way I behave?
- What action do I want to take at this time?

"The Feminine in the Workplace"

The Rose Goddesses
(or the Affirmation of Female Talent)

This collage was great fun to do. It's a tongue-in-cheek reference to women in corporations.

CHAPTER SEVEN

MARKETING YOUR TALENT

When you have found your talent and nurtured it into shape, you're ready to share it with the world. This is when the gift that you have been given will become your gift to others. This is the time to harvest all the work you've done, tilling the soil and nourishing your talent. As with any harvest, you may keep some of it for yourself. Many people have hobbies and other enjoyable pastimes that they don't necessarily want to turn into a career. They engage in these activities strictly for the fun of it. That's fine—not all talents have to be applied to your career.

The notion of selling one's talent is often terrifying. It brings up the fear of rejection, challenging our self-confidence. "Will anybody really want to pay for my talent?" The idea of making an enjoyable living tests the old belief that work is a distasteful necessity. It seems impossible that the things we love doing most could be financially rewarding.

The other frightening aspect of marketing is that many do not see themselves as "business people." Being successful in business doesn't mean that we have to give up who we are or be something that we are not. The word *business* is defined as, "The occupation, work or trade in which a person is engaged." It doesn't mean "selling out" or cleverly conning others.

Business offers us an opportunity to share our talent, to "engage" others in what we do. It also means that we apply our talents to the needs of others. To do this we must communicate in a simple and direct manner. We tell others about the service or product we provide and needs we can fill. It's just as simple as that.

WHAT ARE YOU OFFERING?

The first step in business is to clearly define what you are offering. Getting to know your talent (by doing the exercises in this book) has prepared you to identify your products and services. Matching your talents to needs has helped you identify your market.

Companies spend billions of dollars every year on research and development to define and design exactly what it is they are selling. They must articulate their product or service in words before they can take it to the marketplace. If you want to get paid for working your talent, you must think of yourself in the same way. You'll need to answer the same questions that any company does.

- What product or service am I offering?
- Who needs and will pay for what I am offering?
- What am I charging for my product or service?
- How will I reach my market?

Sharing your talent with others depends upon your ability to *articulate* clearly what it is you have to offer. For example, when strangers ask Lucia what she does for a living, instead of rattling off a list of careers and jobs she's had and books she's written, she simply says: "I'm in the self-empowerment business." That usually piques their interest. "Self-empowerment? Sounds interesting, I could use that. What is it *exactly* that you do?" From there Lucia can go into particulars: workshops, lectures, consulting, counseling, self-help books, tapes, etc. The underlying theme of all this activity is the teaching and learning of self-empowerment. The book you're reading is simply one example of the self-empowerment process applied to talent.

Once you can articulate what your talent is, in the most basic and simple terms, you will be heard by others. If your definition of what you are offering is fuzzy, vague or complicated, it will not get people's attention. In career counseling sessions, one of the first questions Lucia asks her clients is: "What are you selling?" People are often very confused about exactly what it is they are offering.

Here are some ways Lucia guides her clients and students out of confusion and into clarity:

> I work with many multi-talented individuals in the arts and entertainment industry. When I ask what they're selling, they often say, "Oh, I can do anything." I point out that such an answer is *the kiss of death* in marketing.
>
> I tell them, "If you want to get paid for working your talent, you must have something tangible to sell—a service or product that is identifiable. Trying to sell 'anything' will get you nowhere. As a potential client or customer or employer, I can't buy 'anything.' I <u>can</u> buy *something*. However, I need to know specifically what that *something* is." The client usually gets the message. Then we get down to identifying specific services or products they want to market.
>
> The other response I often get when I ask clients what they're selling is a 10-minute résumé speech that leaves me completely confused. An inventory of everything you've ever done in your work life is just too much, especially if you are multi-talented. These individuals get focused by answering the question: "Of all the talents and skills you have, what do you want to do at this time in your life?" That usually gets us back on track. What emerges is a clearly articulated statement that can be taken out to the marketplace.

Once we state clearly what we are offering, matching talent to need becomes much easier. There are billions of unfilled needs out there. Which ones are you going to tackle? Which ones fit with your talent? Which ones do you have a burning passion to fill? Those are the *big* questions when it comes to marketing your talent.

> Paul was a very successful architect in both the residential and theatrical arenas. In his residential work, he gained a reputation for building "dream houses." At the peak of his career, Paul faced a family crisis that reshaped his life. His father became terminally ill and unable to continue working in his publishing business. The family was not only dealing with the imminent loss of a loved one but also the possibility of bankruptcy.

Paul's father asked him to take over the publishing company, which was just entering a crucial marketing phase. Paul was overwhelmed. How could he survive in a business that was completely foreign to him? He knew about Peggy's work in talent development and decided to talk with her about the situation. Peggy asked: "What is the purpose of the publishing company?" Paul replied that it was dedicated to publishing inspirational stories assisting young people in building a positive self-image. The message to the youth was "dreams can come true and you can do it." Paul was able to see the connection between the purpose of the publishing company and his own approach to architecture and design. They were both dedicated to making dreams come true.

In reviewing Paul's talents, Peggy pointed out that he was a builder who understood how to organize and produce a product. These were the same skills he needed to guide the family publishing effort. When asked what the company sold, Paul said: "We sell the stuff that dreams are made of." This idea formed the basis of their marketing campaign. After leading the company for several successful years, Paul recently retired from the family business and is currently designing a new life and environment for himself.

The following activity is extremely useful for focusing and marketing talent. It is a simple, graphic method for taking an overview of all your talents and skills, combining and re-combining them into a marketable "package" that meets identifiable needs.

Packaging My Talent

MATERIALS: Talent Journal and felt pens

1. With your dominant hand, write about the talents or skills you have developed.

2. With your non-dominant hand, draw a picture or chart of your talent assets, including training and experience. Show each talent separately. At the bottom of your picture, write a clear statement of the areas or fields in which you can market your talents. (See example that follows.)

As a kid, I wanted to be a major league baseball player. I played ball all through high school and won a baseball scholarship to a university. I played all through college and won the National Championship College World Series. Also, my parents hosted professional baseball players, so I had a lot of exposure to the pros and what it took to play pro ball. I got a first-hand look at my dream.

I was working for a fitness company through a college internship. So I had immersed myself in sports by the time I was a senior in college. I was making many of my childhood fantasies come true.

I got a degree in business and went on to get my master's in sport management. I didn't become a pro baseball player. I had learned what my limitations were. There were many things going on in the profession that didn't appeal to me, like self-promotion and politics; but I had other talents and I loved sports.

So I continued working with the fitness companies in sales and I eventually became a certified personal trainer for club trainers. My talent for managing has helped me tremendously and, although I'm not a natural salesman, my love of sports and the people in sports has brought out my sales ability.

I used to think that I sold equipment, but I have come to realize that I sell *health*. I help the elderly get stronger, people stay younger and athletes reach their full potential. I help to improve human performance. I love my work.

='s SPORTS EQUIPMENT.
     BUSINESS SELLING
     HEALTH AND WELL-
            Being

As you identify the talents you want to market, it is imperative that you state your product and service briefly. For that reason, writing down what you are selling is extremely valuable. Keep practicing until you can say it in a sentence. The next activity is one that you can repeat on a regular basis to keep clarifying what you are currently selling.

What I'm Offering

MATERIALS: Talent Journal and felt pens

1. With your dominant hand, list your talents. For each talent, complete the following sentence 25 times: "What I am selling is . . ." Write quickly without thinking about it too much. If you have many talents and abilities, include them all. Write one sentence each for each talent. For example:

Management talent

- What I'm selling is *love of and skill in organizing people.*
- What I'm selling are *good communication skills.*
- What I'm selling is *experience in money management.*
- What I'm selling is *skill in managing people and money.*

2. Go back over your list and underline the ones that ring true.

3. Write one sentence that best states what you are selling. Revise and rework the sentence as often as you like. When you are happy with your statement, copy it on file cards. Put them in places where you can see them frequently (in your car, on your desk, wherever you spend much time). Memorize it, affirm it, use it to articulate to others what you are marketing.

What I am selling is:

safety
mechanical parts
technology
doing things right
good will
performance
reliable workmanship
clean environment
efficiency
faith in workmanship
information
positive attitude
customer involvement

As a mechanic, what I am selling is a clean environment and reliable workmanship.

What I'm selling is:

- a technique for realizing your dreams
- a way to listen to your internal images
- a new way to reach goals
- dreams come true
- your inner power coming out
- your sub-conscious expressing itself
- a way of becoming your true self
- a program to become authentic
- a simple way to realize your truest nature
- how to get in touch with your joy
- ways to visualize yourself having everything you want
- methods for visualizing your goals in reality
- methods for visualizing and tapping into your greatest potential

- ways to visualize & realize your goals & objectives

What I am selling is a method for tapping into your full potential through visualization.

How Much Do You Want?

The second big question in business is: "How much do you charge?" This is where many people feel stumped. They are usually venturing into foreign territory with their newly emerging talent. They haven't got a clue about what to charge. Sometimes they don't have confidence in themselves and may hesitate to charge anything. This is where the Inner Critic jumps out and starts trashing the whole enterprise. "Are you kidding? Nobody is going to pay good money for that." If this happens, just go back and do some earlier exercises. Turn to your Talent Fairy Godmother or to your Talent as Healer and Guide. Be good to yourself. Call someone in your support system and ask for some encouragement.

When you feel ready to put a price on your product or service, there are some simple steps you can take. Do a cost and time analysis of your work. Find out how much money and time it takes to produce what you are selling. How much profit do you want to make? What will you have to charge to cover your costs and make a profit?

Another thing you must do is market research. Ask around and find out what others are charging for similar services or products. Find produce what you are selling. If the cost of production is far too high given the market conditions, you may want to create something less costly.

It is not within our scope here to go into detail on marketing and pricing. We simply want to paint a picture with broad brushstrokes. There are many good seminars, books and computer software on various aspects of marketing, selling, negotiating, collecting, etc. In addition to these kinds of resources, we strongly suggest you find a mentor who can give you some seasoned advice. We'll speak more about mentors later in this chapter. Make it your business to learn about business. You'll be much happier and more successful if you do.

Whom Are You Selling To?

The third big question in business is: "Who wants what I am offering and is willing to pay for it?" The second part of that question is very important. There may be many people who want what you have, but if they can't pay for it, then you can't sell it to them. That is not to say that you can't donate your talent when you wish. Such generous sharing is a great way to develop talent and we recommend it. Realistically, most of us have to make a living. There's nothing wrong with getting paid for what you do. It's the way the world works. The point is you have something to offer.

Marketing to the Needs

One test of creativity in marketing is to look for needs that other people have not addressed. In doing the journal activities about needs, you have been preparing yourself to address needs in your marketing strategy. Some people need what you're offering, but they don't realize it's available. Once you find these people and tell them what you're offering, they're likely to be receptive. Lucia identified a need while doing career counseling with several people being laid off by a small manufacturing firm.

> In our sessions, these people all said being laid off was a relief. The suspense had been killing them. Morale at the company was so low that it was downright depressing to be there. Now, they could get on with their lives. Also they were concerned about friends who were still working there. This was a switch because those who are still employed usually feel sorry for those who have been laid off.

> I began thinking about the situation. There was an obvious need for *improving morale within the company*. I contacted a manager and we met to discuss his concerns. He was the first to admit that both morale and productivity were extremely low. I suggested creative problem-solving groups to motivate the staff and build leadership skills. At his request, I submitted a proposal that was accepted. Selecting a small group of the most proactive managers and staff, I conducted weekly sessions. We began brainstorming solutions and got the president's support to implement them. Morale improved dramatically and we turned the situation around within a few months. What · followed was a period of unprecedented and rapid growth. These team members went on to become executives in the newly revived company.

The company Lucia consulted for didn't know they needed "post-termination team-building." No such programs existed at that time. They are now becoming more common. The managers were troubled about the situation, but didn't know where to turn. The employees' "post-layoff blues" remained a problem until our team innovated a tailor-made program to meet the company's specific needs. This type of creative marketing is the stuff entrepreneurship is made of. Obviously, there has to be a match between your talent and the need. When there is, the result can be pure magic. The entrepreneur in us can awaken when necessity calls.

Judy had a longstanding career on Broadway. She had many friends and loved organizing parties. Her two favorite aspects of putting these events together were selecting the catering services and live entertainment. In the late 1980s there was a slump in the theater industry. Many of Judy's associates were convinced that theater in the United States was nearly dead.

Faced with dwindling work in entertainment, Judy decided to start a catering business. Up to that time catering for parties and events was done by people in food services. The entertainment aspect of these events was handled by booking agents. No one was putting the two together. This ambitious young woman created a winning combination: catering and live entertainment. Her customers were delighted because she offered two high-quality services in one simple package. Judy was thrilled because she was able to employ her friends in the entertainment industry. It has been a highly successful enterprise.

When matching talent to need, the key factor is communication. Can you clearly identify the need, articulate it in a way that invites agreement? If the person doesn't agree that he or she has a need, there is nothing further to discuss. Many individuals and companies are in complete denial about their needs. Their official line is: "Everything's fine. We don't have those problems here." If you run into this, thank them for their consideration and move on. Don't waste time that would be better spent pursuing other possibilities. Every time you share an observation you plant a seed. You may have to plant many seeds before one takes hold. It's natural to feel discouraged when your suggestions or ideas are rejected. *Staying* discouraged detours you from your goal. Cultivate your seeds and in time, some of them will grow. Expect some wonderful surprises. Things may not always turn out the way you expected them to, but often they turn out *better*. Patience is the secret ingredient.

If you are selling your services to a company, as a consultant or prospective employee, it is advisable (wherever possible) to find an *inside contact*. The ideal scenario is that you find someone in-house who believes in you and knows that the company needs what you are offering. This person can coach you on the company's specific needs and how best to present yourself to them. This kind of "insider" is motivated to bring you in. He or she wants the company to benefit from your services. In addition, if you do a good job your contact will look good.

Finding an inside contact who is motivated and influential enough to assist you in this way is not always possible. However, if you set it as a goal, you are more likely to achieve it. Many people we've counseled hadn't thought about looking for such an ally within the company. When they've set their minds to finding one, they've often been quite successful.

There's an old saying: "Anyone in the world is only three phone calls away." That's what networking is all about. One contact leads to another, and another and another. We could tell you hundreds of stories about "coincidental" meetings or casual conversations that led to an inside contact in a targeted company. Sometimes it gets really convoluted and almost comical. Your neighbor could be the mother of the president of a company you have your eye on. You might find that your mentor went to school with a manager you've been trying to contact. Her personal referral might open a door that seemed shut.

If you are approaching potential employers for full-time work, know what you are offering in relation to what they are "buying." When interviewing for the job, ask a lot of questions about the position. Your task is to match your talents with their needs. Exactly what is the position that they want to fill? What talents and skills are they looking for? What problems do they need to solve? It is not in your best interest to declare that you will "do anything to get in the door." Employers are not interviewing for "anything." They are looking for someone with particular abilities that will eventually be evaluated in performance reviews.

Marketing does not end once you are employed. No matter where you are in a company's hierarchy, knowing your skills and talents will assist you in successfully getting the assignments you want. Performance reviews that determine raises, merit increases, bonuses and promotions provide you with valuable feedback about your "marketability." They let you know if you are meeting the needs, if you are cultivating your talent and where you need to grow.

Making sure you are matching your talent to needs at all times is one way to stay marketable. In this way you can be ready for any job change that may take place. Whether you are a freelancer or full-time employee, knowing what you offer and who needs it is the best "job security" there is.

Whom I'm Selling To

MATERIALS: Talent Journal and felt pens

1. With your dominant hand, write out your statement from the previous exercise: What are you selling?

2. With your non-dominant hand, make a list of the categories of people who need what you are offering.

3. Draw a picture or make a collage of yourself successfully selling your service or product to people who need it.

What I am selling is:

I engage others in art processes that are specially tailored for their ages, abilities and goals. I am offering art as an essential tool for self-empowerment, self-esteem and personal growth.

I am selling to:

Individuals, groups or organizations who:
- prefer or require non-traditional, informal learning (in their home or location other than public settings).
- want or need a one-on-one learning experience.
- may not have easy access to art (homebound, disabled, terminally ill, aged).
- have always wanted to try art but were afraid.
- are looking for an outlet for creative expression.

- want to learn to draw and paint.
- are looking for innovative ways to enhance creativity and problem-solving.

Identifying what I am selling is hard but if I can do it, all the rest is easy.

I decided to just write out my thoughts about the question of whom I'm selling to. My husband and I are both professional musicians. We also have backgrounds in theater. Our income in music has never been quite enough, so we've always had other part-time work: in restaurants, offices, telephone sales, etc.

A few months ago we started putting on birthday parties for our nieces and nephews. We did it just for fun, never expecting any financial rewards. Dressing up as the child's favorite fairy tale characters, we acted out stories the kids could participate in. Sort of like "story theater." We were such a hit that some of the kids have talked their parents into hiring us to entertain at *their* birthday parties.

We've decided to start a party business, but we're not exactly sure how to go about it. How much should we charge? Is there enough of a demand so that this could become our alternative income source? Guess we'll never find out if we don't try it. We aren't limited to children my nieces and nephews know. Some other possibilities are: churches, nursery schools, elementary schools, summer camps, youth programs, the local libraries. Maybe we could even perform at the children's hospital.

I guess we should put together a brochure describing what we do . . . get endorsements from kids (with their ages). This could really be fun and solve our problem of uninteresting part-time jobs.

Reaching the Market

You may not have realized it, but the journal activities you have been doing throughout this book were preparing you to step out into the world with your talent. You have been following good business planning procedures: knowing your assets (talent), developing them and then marketing them. In reaching the market, you'll be doing what any business does: getting the word out to potential buyers through some form of advertising. A résumé is a form of advertising. So is a flyer posted on a bulletin board or a telephone call to a prospective employer, client or customer.

In presenting your product or service, it is important to have some type of visual piece to hand out or send through mail or e-mail. Résumés are the traditional "advertising piece" used to seek employment. Depending on what you are marketing, you may need more than one résumé. If you are doing freelance work or selling your services or products directly to the public, you'll need a business card and a larger information piece of some kind. The journal activities you just did are an excellent preparation for creating a brochure, flyer or ad. In these days of desktop publishing, creating information pieces has become very easy and inexpensive. A statement of *what you offer and who will benefit from it* is the basis for such a promotional piece. There should also be information about *who you are and why you are qualified to offer this service.* This is how you will engender trust.

Networking

The term "networking" is currently used to describe word-of-mouth advertising. Broadcasting your intent to everyone you know is a good way to begin. You never know who is going to lead you to someone with a need you can fill. Why is word-of-mouth advertising the best? First of all, it's inexpensive. Making phone calls, meeting with people and getting referrals are all very cost-effective ways to reach your market. Secondly, it's based on trust. If a friend that I trust recommends your product or service, I'm far more likely to take you seriously. If my friend is a satisfied customer of yours, I'll want to look into what you are offering. The adage, "It's not what you know, but who you know," is partially true. We think it's both. Certainly you need a quality product or service, but *who* you know makes a huge difference.

A good way to prepare yourself for networking is to identify everyone you know in categories, such as family, friends, etc. This will form the basis of your contact file.

Networking Inventory

MATERIALS: Talent Journal and felt pens

1. With your dominant hand, list the categories of people in your network of friends, loved ones and acquaintances.

Some categories are: Family, friends, neighbors, co-workers or former co-workers, employers or former employers, professional associates, hobby pals, professionals whose services you use (attorney, physician, etc.), service workers in your community, alumni from school, community organizations, volunteer groups, etc. (You can also make a chart of this list, as shown below.)

2. After your list is complete, make file cards or a computer database with names, addresses, phone numbers and space for pertinent information. In this space, record comments about meetings or phone calls you have with the person. What course of action suggests itself from this information? Include schedules and your next steps, and put them on your master calendar.

3. Set priorities and start contacting people. Aim for getting three referrals from everyone you contact. This way your network will expand rapidly. You can do follow-up with your business card, brochure or other visual material.

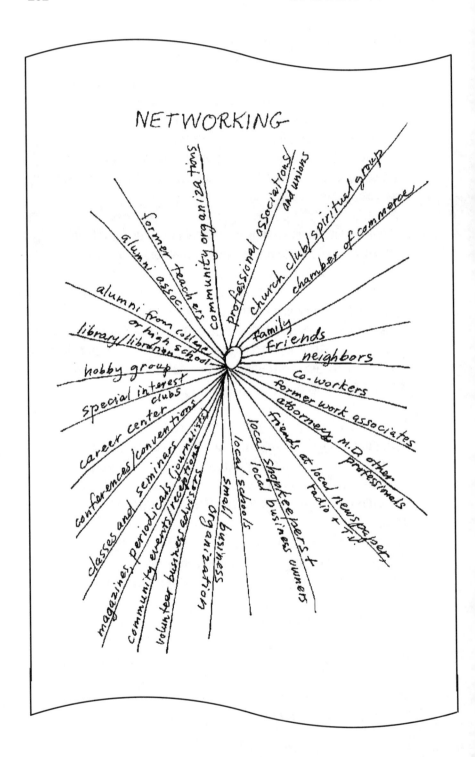

It is easier and less threatening to begin networking by contacting those who are supportive. There will be less fear of rejection to deal with. You will have to determine who these people are. Pull their names from your file and set up a networking schedule. Remember to get three referrals from everyone you contact. Put these marketing appointments in your calendar and then set about to implement your plan.

After doing some one-on-one contact work, you can begin networking in group situations. Check your category list for ideas on groups. Have some printed information, such as a business card or brochure, to hand out. Remember to follow up with those who show an interest in what you are offering. They may not be able to buy what you are selling right now, but they may in the future. Also, they may know someone who is a potential customer or client.

Successful marketing requires consistent effort. Put "marketing" on your calendar. Use your marketing time to:

- Make calls
- Send follow-up information, letters, etc.
- Produce printed pieces or e-mail
- Go to club meetings, receptions, events where you can make contacts
- Take classes in marketing, business, etc.
- Read up on marketing, sales, negotiating, etc.
- Do market research by reviewing classified ads and other advertising
- Brainstorm more marketing ideas

To motivate yourself to market your talent, it is crucial that you develop a support system. This is essential. Support starts with one other person and can grow into a group. Here are some possibilities. We encourage you to expand on our suggestions.

A TALENT MENTOR

High on your list of marketing resources will be a Talent Mentor. This is someone in your community who has already marketed the kind of product or service you are selling. Select someone who can provide inspiration, information and guidance. If you're an aspiring entrepreneur, you might choose a mentor who owns his or her own business. A wonderful way to seek mentoring is to offer some kind of assistance to your mentor. This is the basis for the apprentice system.

> Leila, a tax accountant, wanted to develop her talent as a financial analyst. She did an exchange with one of her clients, Frank, who was a successful financial analyst. Following Frank's advice and encouragement, Leila returned to school and got her MBA degree. In return for tutoring, Leila did Frank's taxes for free. Upon graduation, Leila was offered a position in Frank's firm. They have continued to have a mutually beneficial work relationship.

If you don't know where to find a mentor, start with someone you do know. It is advisable to talk to people in a related field.

> When Lucia decided to explore a career in art therapy, she called a psychologist she knew and asked for a referral. The very first referral was a pioneering art therapist who turned out to be the perfect mentor. She and Lucia had similar backgrounds in art and film. They struck up an immediate rapport. This woman was her guide and teacher throughout Lucia's graduate studies.

The idea is to find someone who has been where you want to go. Get some exposure to reality and compare it to your expectations and dreams.

PERSONAL PRESENTATION

Articulating what you do is a key factor in marketing your talent. How you speak, dress, move, use language and visual aids when presenting your talent are crucial. We have found that coaching in personal presentation is indispensable. One of our teachers has been Arthur Joseph, an internationally known voice coach. Arthur points out that, "One's voice instantly reaches out and connects us with others."

Arthur's system, Vocal Awareness, helps people express who they really are without embarrassment or hesitation. He seeks to free his students from the entrapments of stress, poor posture, lazy vocal habits and self-consciousness. If you want to bring forth the natural voice that speaks for your talent, consider getting his book, *The Sound of the Soul: Discovering the Power of Your Voice*. He has also produced audiotapes on Vocal Awareness (See Resources).

Improvisational theater classes are another valuable and fun way to prepare yourself for marketing. Improv training helps you become comfortable in front of people and to "think on your feet." It accesses the part of your brain where words flow and creativity flourishes. If you want to contact the "salesperson within," we urge you to consider taking a class or workshop in improvisational theater.

We have both benefited greatly from studying improv and from personal presentation coaching. We have also witnessed unbelievable transformations in people who surmounted their fear of public speaking and selling through these methods. Many of these were highly creative individuals in their area of expertise, but had no experience making personal presentations. After being coached, many of them became such effective presenters that they moved into positions of leadership at their jobs. Some of them even went on to start their own companies.

We strongly suggest that you explore classes, workshops or seminars for developing abilities related specifically to marketing your talent. Toastmasters, adult education and college extension courses are plentiful and usually inexpensive. Private workshops and seminars on topics related to personal presentation, marketing, speaking, etc. are also available. Check the newspapers, local directories or bulletin boards in your community. You might also want to research local organizations and clubs, such as Women in Business, Entrepreneurs, etc. Many of these organizations offer special workshops for members on marketing. You may be surprised at the wealth of resources you'll find.

TEAM POWER

Marketing your talent involves communicating with people. A great place to practice communicating your talent is by dialoging with others. Doing this can help you get the most out of the principles and activities in this book. Interaction with others who are supportive provides a wonderful testing ground for articulating clearly the talent that you are offering.

Many people who attend Lucia's workshops say: "Reading the book was great, but being with other people working on the same issues—*that* really got me started. Afterward, I felt much more motivated to do the activities and apply the information."

There are several places to find support. The traditional approach has been to seek career counseling or seminars. These services usually involve professional help and a fee. Beyond finding a Talent Mentor, here are some ways to get support:

- Find a Talent Buddy
- Join a support group
- Start a support group

Talent Buddies

Having someone with whom you can develop mutual support is an invaluable part of the process of talent development. We call this a Talent Buddy. The gift of revealing our truth is a double blessing. As we share our dreams and wishes with others, we invite them to support us. In turn, we respectfully listen to others and offer them our support. This non-judgmental atmosphere of mutual recognition and acceptance is highly conducive to nurturing talent.

Find someone you trust who is also committed to developing his or her talent. Talent Buddies can be found in classes, professional organizations, special interest groups and clubs. A like-minded friend, family member, neighbor or co-worker could turn out to be a great Talent Buddy.

Establish a routine for meetings and telephone calls to share your goals and progress with each other. Encourage one another through the inevitable obstacles. Talent Buddies are committed to:

- Helping each other stay focused and on track.
- Giving mutual moral support and encouragement.
- Acting as a sounding board for feelings, wishes, plans and reviews.
- Sharing information, resources, skills and help in emergencies.
- Providing each other with role-modeling and mentoring.
- Celebrating each other's successes.

Darlene, an aspiring management consultant, was preparing a presentation for her first potential client. Caught in the grips of pure stage fright, she called Sharon, her Talent Buddy. Sharon agreed to role-play the client for a "dress rehearsal" that Darlene put on for her. After practicing in this manner for a couple of hours, Darlene felt calmer and more confident. The next day, she met with the client and walked away with her first contract. The two Buddies celebrated Darlene's success by going out to dinner.

Marketing Support System

MATERIALS: Talent Journal and felt pens

1. With your non-dominant hand, draw a diagram or picture of your support system. Write the names of people or groups who can help you market your talent.

2. With your dominant hand, write out what kind of support you want to ask for.

3. With your dominant hand, write out a marketing plan. Implement it!

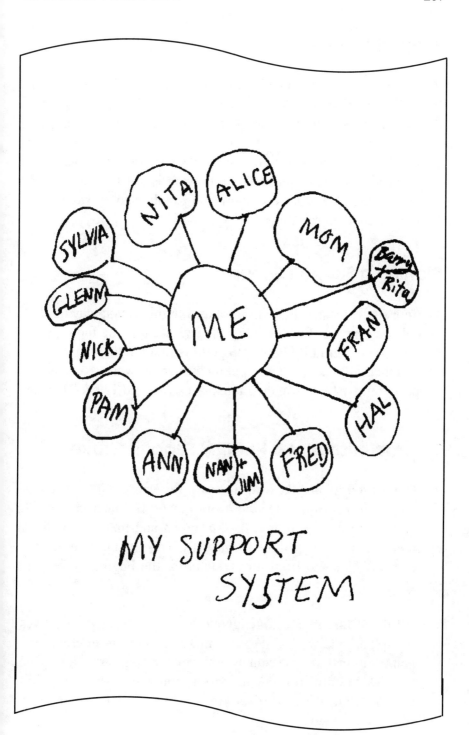

Support Groups

It's often been said that there is power in numbers. This is certainly true when it comes to talent development. We strongly recommend that you consider joining a support group. Look for an appropriate group in your community. If you can't find one, start your own. Whether you join a group that already exists or start a new one, you'll need some guidelines. The following is a list of some of the characteristics of a healthy support group, followed by suggestions for how to conduct meetings.

Starting a Support Group

Starting a talent support group is not as difficult as you may think. If you already have a Talent Buddy, all you need is one more person and you have a group. The whole point is to elicit the help of other like-minded folks who want to put their talent to work. You can find support group members in the same places you find Talent Buddies.

Characteristics of a Healthy Support Group

1. **Composed of people who are safe for you**. "Safe" means *no judgment, pressure or blame* from others. If "inner critics" are on the loose, the group will shut down and members will not feel free to share or to be themselves. This ground rule must be clearly stated up front and restated at the beginning of each session.

2. **A mix of talents and backgrounds**. A variety of perspectives, disciplines and work experience make for a balanced group. It is helpful to include individuals with some background in finance, business administration, invention/innovation or production. People from different disciplines bring a much broader perspective to the group.

3. **An atmosphere of respect and mutual support—democratic, equalitarian, non-hierarchical**. No one member "runs" the group. Each session is facilitated by a different member selected by the group (this is called revolving leadership).

4. **Regularly scheduled, preferably weekly sessions**. This is essential for establishing consistency and commitment. We recommend sessions of two to three hours long and a six-week commitment. Members can recommit to another six-week series if they wish, continuing as long as it is appropriate and productive.

5. **Flexible, allowing the group's size to change depending on the needs of the group**. A new group might start with smaller numbers (five to eight) until everyone feels comfortable with the group dynamics. All you need to do is find two people. Many groups started with three people. If the group is effective, it will be easy to find other members through word-of-mouth. In starting a second cycle of meetings, more members might be added if the group wishes. It is not advisable to bring new members into the group in mid-series. They should wait for a new cycle to begin. The group size should be small enough so that every member has an opportunity to speak in the sharing segments.

To keep your sessions focused, it is advisable to have a written guideline. These should be read at each session. You can use all or part of the above list. You can also add other guidelines that pertain to your particular group. Every decision that is made *for* the group should be made *by* the group. Remember, a democratic process is essential for a truly effective support group.

Structuring Support Group Sessions

1. The chosen leader for the session invites each member of the group to share for three to five minutes. He or she shares one success and one challenge, followed by a statement of personal talent goals for this session.

   For instance: *I am having trouble deciding which of three talents I want to focus on at this time. I love to write. I am good with people. I also like interior decorating. In this session, I would like to get clearer on which of these talents to develop and market first.*

2. The leader assigns one activity from this book. Allow 30 to 45 minutes to do the activity. If an individual prefers to do a different activity from the book, he or she should feel free to do so.

   Four out of five members of one group were having problems developing their talent. They selected an exercise that would help them organize their time, set priorities and make talent appointments for the following week. The fifth member of the group had developed her talent as a freelance editor but was having difficulty marketing. She did an exercise that focused on identifying those people who needed her services.

3. The group should take a 10- to 15-minute break.

4. In the last segment of the session, each member is free to share if he or she wants. There is no pressure; sharing is strictly voluntary. It is very important that there be no cross-talk and no interruptions during this sharing. Each person has the floor for an agreed amount of time, depending on the size of the group (for instance, if the sharing period is 45 minutes and there are five members of the group, each one may have nine minutes to share). The idea is to enable each group member to share if he or she wishes to.

Celebrating

Although supporting each other through the hard times is crucial, it is equally important to celebrate success. We do this by having parties, outings, field trips and other special treats. One group celebrated successes with special potluck dinners. Another group celebrated with a toast at the end of the session. A pair of Talent Buddies honored their achievements with special gifts. They gave things to each other such as a miniature Oscar, a parchment "talent award" inscribed in calligraphy and a custom-made bumper sticker.

CONGRATULATIONS!

We want to extend to you our heartfelt congratulations for your willingness to identify, develop and market your innate gifts. We appreciate the courage and work it takes to embrace this journey with commitment. We know it is an ongoing process that bears fruit along the way. Perhaps the greatest reward is the discovery of who you are, how you behave and what actions to take in putting your talent to work. Our wish is that you find the joy and rewards that come from honoring your talent and expressing your full potential.

Peggy Van Pelt

Lucia Capacchione

RESOURCES

RESOURCES

Books

Anderson, Nancy. *Working with Passion.* San Rafael, Calif.: New
World Library, 1995.

Atchity, Kenneth. *The Mercury Transition: Career-Change
Empowerment Through Entrepreneurship.* Stamford, Conn.:
Longmeadow Press, 1994.

Baber, Anne, and Lynne Wayman. *How to Fireproof Your Career.*
New York: Bantam, 1995.

Bolles, Richard. *What Color Is Your Parachute?* Berkeley, Calif.:
Ten Speed Press, 1995.

Bridges, William. *Job Shift.* Reading, Mass.: Addison-Wesley, 1994.

Capacchione, Lucia. *The Creative Journal: The Art of Finding
Yourself.* Athens, Ohio: Ohio University/Swallow Press,
1979. Smaller format edition: Van Nuys, Calif.: Newcastle
Publishing, 1989.

_____. *The Power of Your Other Hand.* Van Nuys, Calif.:
Newcastle Publishing, 1988.

_____. *Recovery of Your Inner Child.* New York: Simon &
Schuster, 1991.

Edwards, Paul, and Sarah Edwards. *Finding Your Perfect Work.*
New York: Tarcher/Putnam, 1996.

_____. *Making It on Your Own.* New York: Tarcher/Putnam, 1991.

_____. *Working from Home.* New York: Tarcher/Putnam, 1994.

Felsher, Murray. *Working Alone.* New York: Berkeley Books, 1994.

Frohbieter-Mueller, Jo. *Stay Home and Mind Your Own Business.* White Hall, Va.: Betterway Publications, 1987.

Hawken, Paul. *Growing a Business.* New York: Fireside/Simon & Schuster, 1988.

Joseph, Arthur. *The Sound of the Soul: Discovering the Power of Your Voice.* Deerfield Beach, Fla.: Health Communications, Inc., 1996.

McWhinney, Will, and Eleanor F. McCulley. *Creating Paths of Change.* Venice, Calif.: Enthusion, Inc., 1993.

Sinetar, Marsha. *Do What You Love, The Money Will Follow.* New York: Dell, 1989.

_____. *To Build the Life You Want, Create the Work You Love.* New York: St. Martin's, 1995.

Winter, Barbara J. *Making a Living Without a Job.* New York: Bantam, 1993.

Audiotapes

Capacchione, Lucia. *The Wisdom of Your Other Hand.* Boulder, Colo.: Sounds True, set of 5 tapes.

Joseph, Arthur. *Vocal Awareness.* Boulder, Colo.: Sounds True, set of 6 tapes.

Share the Magic of Chicken Soup

Chicken Soup for the Soul™
101 Stories to Open the Heart
and Rekindle the Spirit

The #1 *New York Times* bestseller and ABBY award-winning inspirational book that has touched the lives of millions. Whether you buy it for yourself or as a gift to others, you're sure to enrich the lives of everyone around you with this affordable treasure.

Code 262X trade paperback $12.95
Code 2913 hardcover $24.00
Code 3812 large print $16.95

A 2nd Helping of Chicken Soup for the Soul™
101 More Stories to Open the Heart and
Rekindle the Spirit

This rare sequel accomplishes the impossible—it is as tasty as the original, and still fat-free. If you enjoyed the first *Chicken Soup for the Soul,* be warned: it was merely the first course in an uplifting grand buffet. These stories will leave you satisfied and full of self-esteem, love and compassion.

Code 3316 trade paperback $12.95
Code 3324 hardcover $24.00
Code 3820 large print $16.95

A 3rd Serving of Chicken Soup for the Soul™
101 More Stories to Open the Heart
and Rekindle the Spirit

The latest addition to the *Chicken Soup for the Soul* series is guaranteed to put a smile in your heart. Learn through others the important lessons of love, parenting, forgiveness, hope and perseverance. This tasty literary stew will stay with you long after you've put the book down.

Code 3790 trade paperback $12.95
Code 3804 hardcover $24.00
Code 4002 large print $16.95

Available at your favorite bookstore or call 1-800-441-5569 for Visa or MasterCard orders. Prices do not include shipping and handling. Your response code is **BKS**.

HCI's Business Self-Help Books

What You Want, Wants You
How to Get Out of Your Rut
Debra Jones

People in the 1990s are reevaluating their lifestyles as never before. With the stability of tenured positions in large corporations becoming a thing of the past, many workers are rethinking their career choices to be more in tune with what they really want to do. Here Debra Jones, marketing whiz extraordinaire, gives you a game plan for digging yourself out of the quagmire of indecision and hopelessness in order to find your life path. An inspiring book that will leave you revitalized.

Code 3677 . . . .**$9.95**

Networking Success
How to Turn Business & Financial Relationships into Fun & Profit
Anne Boe

Networking is the business tool of the 1990s—(a must for keeping the competitive edge that separates the successful from the unsuccessful. Along with networking's unquestioned value in business, it's also useful in personal relationships. Here master networker Anne Boe describes ideas for developing, nurturing and growing your relationships, financial contacts and career networks for peak performance on and off the job.

Code 3650 . . . .**$12.95**

How to Get What You Want from Almost Anybody
Your Self-Defense Consumer Guide
T. Scott Gross

The author gives his secrets for dealing with everyone from waiters, salesclerks and service attendants, to car salesmen and real estate agents. With an emphasis on the importance of being a good customer and having fun without being taken, T. Scott Gross explains: why you must know—and expect—what you want; what the proven strategies for getting good service are; how to effectively complain about and correct poor service; and how to get the best deal (or steal) possible.

Code 3715 . . . . **$10.95**

Available at your favorite bookstore or call 1-800-441-5569 for Visa or MasterCard orders. Prices do not include shipping and handling.
Your response code is **BKS.**

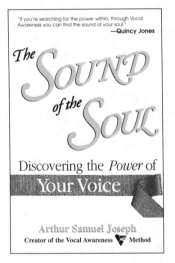